D0038370

THE NEW SCIENCE OF LEARNING

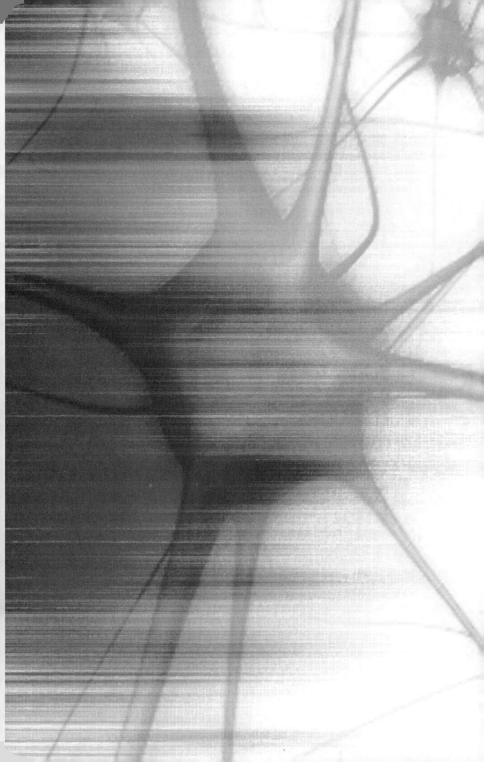

Terry Doyle and
Todd Zakrajsek

THE NEW
SCIENCE OF
LEARNING

How to Learn in Harmony
With Your Brain

Foreword by Jeannie H. Loeb

STERLING, VIRGINIA

COPYRIGHT © 2013 BY
STYLUS PUBLISHING, LLC.

Published by Stylus Publishing, LLC.
22883 Quicksilver Drive
Sterling, Virginia 20166-2102

All rights reserved. No part of this book may be reprinted
or reproduced in any form or by any electronic, mechanical,
or other means, now known or hereafter invented, including
photocopying, recording, and information storage and
retrieval, without permission in writing from the publisher.

Library of Congress Cataloging-in-Publication Data
The CIP data for this book has been applied for.

13-digit ISBN: 978-1-62036-008-8 (cloth)
13-digit ISBN: 978-1-62036-009-5 (paper)
13-digit ISBN: 978-1-62036-010-1 (library networkable e-edition)
13-digit ISBN: 978-1-62036-011-8 (consumer e-edition)

Printed in the United States of America.

All first editions printed on acid-free paper
that meets the American National Standards Institute
Z39-48 Standard.

Bulk Purchases

Quantity discounts are available for use in workshops and for staff
development.
Call 1-800-232-0223

First Edition, 2013

11

For my parents, Bill and Winnie, my favorite teachers.

—Terry Doyle

For my students, who were also some of my best teachers.

—Todd Zakrajsek

CONTENTS

ACKNOWLEDGMENTS

I want to begin by thanking my amazing wife, Professor Julie Doyle, for the hundreds of hours of discussion she had with me about students' learning and what could be done to enhance or improve it. I also want to thank my son, Brendan, who was a sounding board for many of the ideas expressed in this book. I need to thank Michael Graham Richard for allowing us to use his work in our chapter on mindset and the people at Posit Science for allowing us to use one of their pictures to help illustrate the memory-forming process in the brain. I also want to thank Dr. Jeannie Loeb for her contributions to the science of this book and for her willingness to write the foreword. In addition, I need to thank John von Knorring at Stylus for his editing and many ideas about how to make this book better. Finally, I want to thank my students at Ferris State University who read draft chapters and offered great feedback on how to tailor the book to meet the needs of college students.

Terry Doyle

I must give almost total credit for everything I write to my wife, Debra; my three children, Emma, Mary, and Kathryn; and my grandson, Matthew. They have listened to endless stories, shared their learning experiences, and been the inspiration for essentially all I know about how people learn. I don't have the words to adequately thank my colleague and good friend Jeannie Loeb for both writing the foreword for this book and allowing me to talk through so many issues and ideas when I needed a sounding board. I would like to also acknowledge John von Knorring for making this project what it is and for his keen eye in editing the many exceptional books published by Stylus, which have shaped much of what we all know about student learning and faculty development. I would like to thank my students for their eagerness to learn, my faculty friends for their willingness to share, and my colleagues for providing a safe place to play. Finally, thanks to all of you who are expanding your minds by pursuing higher education. It is a wicked challenge at times, but necessary if we are going to find our way.

Todd Zakrajsek

FOREWORD

This book is a must-read for students who want time both to "have a life" and to improve the way they learn. Too frequently, students are left on their own to navigate through a variety of study and learning strategies, which are often not based on brain research. As coauthor Todd Zakrajsek, or Dr. Z, as he is known to his students, often says, "Higher education is odd in that we don't typically teach teachers how to teach, students how to learn, or administrators how to lead." As a result, more than a few students end up with methods that are ineffective or even an impediment to learning.

Neuroscientists know so much about how the brain learns best. Unfortunately, they do not usually present their discoveries to those involved with teaching, and neither instructors nor students have the time to sift through the voluminous amount of scientific research currently available. Fortunately, Terry Doyle and Todd Zakrajsek have done the sifting for you, as Terry says, in an effort to help students "stop swimming upstream in their learning." *The New Science of Learning: How to Learn in Harmony With Your Brain* highlights and summarizes some of the most recent and impactful insights regarding learning and memory. In particular, it helps students to better understand the learner-centered approach to teaching and learning, a movement that is slowly becoming the norm in higher education. It not only is packed with practical applications of current brain research but also describes *why* applying these skills and strategies works in light of the brain's design.

You don't want to miss being a part of this revolutionary approach to learning!

It is particularly fitting that our latest understanding of how the brain learns is shared with you by Terry and Todd, as each have been intimately involved with higher education for decades. In his 41 years as an educator, Terry has received awards for his outstanding teaching at Ferris State University—where he is currently professor of reading— three times; he has published two other books on teaching and students' learning, one of which was recognized in *The Chronicle of Higher Education*'s Selected New Books on Higher Education; he has been senior and chief instructor for faculty development for 12 of the 16 years he has been helping faculty members to become more effective instructors; and he has given numerous presentations and workshops on teaching and learning strategies that are consistent with scientific research. In fact, it was after one of these presentations that Terry approached Todd about writing this book.

Todd, in turn, is a heavyweight in the arena of teaching and learning, particularly faculty development. He has written numerous publications and is the founding, inaugural, and executive director of faculty development centers at several institutions, including the University of North Carolina–Chapel Hill, where he is currently associate professor in the Department of Family Medicine, associate director of Fellowship Programs, and teaching consultant in the Academy of Educators. He too has given countless presentations and workshops on teaching and learning (usually as a plenary or keynote speaker) and is likely one of the few who can claim to have given workshops in 42 states, as well as at a growing number of international venues.

I have had the great fortune of attending some of Terry's and Todd's presentations at university and college teaching conferences, and I can tell you that they not only have much teaching wisdom to share but are also quite humorous and charismatic presenters. For those of you who may not have the opportunity to see them present in person, *The New Science of Learning: How to Learn in Harmony With Your Brain* is a great way of gleaning some of their most recent and critical tips on becoming a more efficient and effective learner. Following their advice, in turn, will allow one to have more time to "have a life."

Jeannie Loeb

Jeannie H. Loeb, PhD
Senior Lecturer, Behavioral Neuroscience in Psychology
University of North Carolina–Chapel Hill

INTRODUCTION

Learning is a complicated practice. Several thousand years ago, the primary obligation of the human brain was to figure out how to find food, avoid getting eaten by a predator (including finding a safe place to sleep), and find a mate. Now, in addition to those basic human functions, our brains are inundated with other facts and tasks that need to be learned. Unfortunately, the evolution of a biological structure such as the brain does not allow for change at a pace as rapid as that at which our society is currently changing. Just imagine how much more complicated the human life has become in the last 80 years, approximately three generations. College alone is a challenge that many of our great-grandfathers never faced. The good news is that although our brains have not changed significantly in the past several hundred years, our understanding of how our brains work is light-years ahead of where we were only a short time ago.

New insights into how the human brain learns make it clear that many of the learning practices that faculty used in the past, and that students continue to use, are highly inefficient, ineffective, or just plain wrong. Better learning does not always require more effort or more time; rather one need only effectively align how the brain naturally learns with the demands of the college classroom. This book succinctly outlines several easily adapted changes that will significantly enhance your college experience by helping you learn *how to learn in harmony with your brain.*

Why is it particularly important to learn how to learn as effectively and efficiently as possible? The onslaught of new information, innovation, and challenges facing our world is not going to diminish. College students today face a new world order in which global competition for jobs is the norm rather than the exception. India and China have twice as many honor students as the United States has people (Herbold, 2008). These honor students will be seeking the same professional positions that you are seeking. A 2010 study by Georgetown University revealed that 55–65% (depending on the state you live in) of all jobs in the United States will require postsecondary education by 2018. This is up from 28% in 1973 (Carnevale, Smith, & Strohl, 2010). Thus, as a student in college right now, you are a member of the first generation in U.S. history made up of people who must be lifelong learners in order to remain employed. It is essential that you become a highly efficient and effective learner who retains knowledge and skills for a lifetime, not just for a test, if you are to compete successfully on the world stage.

ʬ

This brief book, based on what is currently known about how the human brain learns, will help you to change how you prepare to learn, make your learning easier and more effective, and more successfully recall newly learned material whenever you need it. Taking the time to read and reflect on the material in this book will be one of the best decisions you will have ever made as a learner. At this point you might be thinking, "There must be a million books out there about how to study and be successful in college." This is not a book designed to teach you specific study skills, learning strategies, or techniques for improving your attitude toward learning. This book instead explains research about how the human brain learns in a way that is easy to understand and act upon. This book gives you a foundation on which you can build study skills as needed, but with a much better understanding of why and how those skills can be best implemented. As just one example, did you know that neuroscientists have shown that understanding of new material and subsequent recall of that material is enhanced if you don't take classes back-to-back? The human brain needs downtime between different learning experiences in order to process and begin to make memories of the newly experienced material. The brain needs to work to learn new things, and we need to give it time to do that work. Neuroscientist Lila Davachi of New York University said, "Students would be better off taking a coffee break where they just chat with friends for an hour following a college class— it would actually be better for their learning" (Davachi, Tambini, & Ketz, 2010). Strategically implemented leisure time in which the brain is not processing a lot of new material, when not overdone, is actually an effective part of the learning process.

The authors of this book have a singular goal for anyone reading or listening to this material: to better understand *how you can learn how to learn in harmony with your brain.* It is not difficult to make the changes suggested in this book. But it is critical. Becoming a skilled and efficient learner will be one of the most important determinants of what you can and will achieve in your lifetime. Our purpose in writing this book is to help you reach your full potential by providing you a simple way to understand the learning process. That simple way will allow you to get to places in your lifetime that people have not even dreamed of yet.

A Special Note to the Reader

As authors we have purposefully written each chapter of this book to be a stand-alone body of information about a certain aspect of the human brain. As a result, some information is repeated in multiple chapters. Also, some information is discussed in multiple chapters because it happens in the brain as a result of different activities or causes. For example, making new memories is affected by sleep (chapter 2), exercise (chapter 3), practice and elaboration (chapter 6), and attention (chapter 8). We believe that the repetition will serve to reinforce important information and that the reader will find it helpful to consider the information in multiple ways.

References

Carnevale, A. P., Smith, N., & Strohl, J. (2010, June). *Projections of jobs and education requirements through 2018.* Washington, DC: Georgetown University, Center for Education and the Workforce. Retrieved from http://www9.georgetown.edu/grad/gppi/hpi/cew/pdfs/FullReport.pdf

Davachi, L., Tambini, A., & Ketz, N. (2010). Enhanced brain correlations during rest are related to memory for recent experiences. *Neuron, 65*(2), 280–290.

Herbold, R. (2008, December). Does the U.S. realize it's in competition? *Think.* Retrieved from http://www.case.edu/magazine/springsummer2010/competition.html

1

A NEW LOOK AT LEARNING

We all learn throughout our lives. We learn how to tie our shoes, the best route to get to the mall, which friends we can trust, how to find the area of a circle, and how to write a research paper. Surprisingly, very few people are taught how to learn. Even college professors, who spend 20 years in the educational system and obtain a PhD, learn by doing what seems best, but rarely by consulting the vast literature on how people learn. If you are in college, or will be heading off to college shortly, you certainly are good at learning, but knowing (a) how your brain learns, (b) which strategies bring about the most learning, and (c) under which circumstances optimal learning occurs is something that can benefit anyone. Helping you to understand and then apply to your own life the research on these three crucial aspects of learning is the purpose of this book.

This is a book about how to *learn in harmony with your brain*. It is now at last possible to write an easy-to-read, research-based book on this topic because 15 years ago scientists began to develop highly effective tools for looking inside the human brain. Thus, today we have a much better understanding of how the most complicated system ever known—the human brain—operates. We have the technology to actually see which areas of the brain are involved when a person thinks about flying, and even to pinpoint where memories of a shopping trip with a favorite cousin are stored. Although neuroscientists' understanding of how the brain works is still far from complete, at a 2010 meeting of neuroscience experts, Dr. James Bibb of the University of Texas Southwestern Medical Center said, "We have accumulated enough knowledge about the mechanisms and molecular underpinnings of cognition at the synaptic and circuit levels to say something about which processes contribute" (as cited in Begley, 2011). Bibb expanded on his statement in a 2010 article in the *Journal of Neuroscience*, in which he and his coauthors indicated that there is finally enough understanding about how learning happens to suggest that the process is wholly different from what most students imagine (Bibb, Mayford, Tsien, & Alberini, 2010). This places us on the front edge of being able to better facilitate learning abilities. In this book, we will share the newest findings with respect to how you might best learn in harmony with your brain.

A New Definition of *Learning*

What does it mean to say you have learned something?

Neuroscience researchers have shown that when you learn something new, there is a physical change in your brain. You have approximately 86 billion brain cells (Randerson, 2012), and when you learn something new, some of your brain cells establish connections with other brain cells to form new networks of cells, which represent the new learning that has taken place. When frequently activated, these new networks have the potential to become long-term memories. In fact, every time you use or practice the newly learned information or skill, the connections between the brain cells get stronger and recalling the information becomes easier. Establishing connections is like blazing a trail, which is a great deal of work. But every time the trail is used, it becomes more established and easier to follow. At the level of neurons, establishing and then maintaining the trail is called long-term potentiation (Ratey, 2001). As a result of long-term potentiation, something that was at one time new to you, such as adding two to five, becomes routine. Long-term potentiation is a neurological description of how habits and long-term memories are formed. Any practiced knowledge, or skill, becomes a more permanent part of your memory and will be easily available to you when you need it, even if you don't need it for weeks or months at a time.

The important message for all learners is that new learning requires a considerable amount of practice and a meaningful connection to other information in order to become a more permanent part of memory. Learning takes energy. You may even find yourself exhausted at the end of the day when you have learned a lot of new material. There are some shortcuts, but never underestimate the energy consumed by your brain when you learn. As challenging as it is to learn when you are excited to learn and enjoy the material, you know that it is even more difficult to learn when you either don't want to learn or are a passive listener rather than an active participant. What neuroscience researchers have made clear is that "the one who does the work does the learning" (Doyle, 2008). The more ways you engage with something that you are learning—such as listening, talking, reading, writing, reviewing, or thinking about the material or skill—the stronger the connections in your brain become and the more likely the new learning will become a more permanent memory.

Neuroscience researchers have also found that to form lasting memories, practice typically needs to happen over extended periods. Psychologists call this the distributed practice effect (Anderson & Pavlik, 2008; Ebbinghaus, 1913). Think about how ridiculous it would be to cram in a long weight-lifting session the night before you need strength. Would you expect to be much stronger the next morning? If you had a race to run, could you cram all your running practices in the day before the meet and expect to set your best time? If you really wanted to be stronger or faster, you would practice a bit every day over a certain period. You would also expect practices to make you tired. The same is true for your brain. To build strong areas of knowledge, distributed practice is important. That said, even when you have learned something, if you don't practice what you have learned the information fades. The same thing happens if you exercise for a while and then stop: the muscle fades. New learning is very much a "use it or lose it" proposition.

All this new research in neuroscience has led to a completely new way of thinking about the teaching and learning process in school called learner-centered teaching (LCT). Not all teachers are using LCT, but every year more do, and that is certainly the direction in which higher education will continue to go. In the LCT model, your teacher's goal is to get you to do as much of the work in the learning process as possible, because the more work your brain does, the greater the number of connections established. More connections in turn increase the likelihood that more permanent memories will be formed. The LCT approach is often uncomfortable for students who are used to having their teachers tell them what to learn and memorizing that information a day or two before the test. The discomfort usually comes from being asked to do more work and to take a more active role in the classroom, rather than just listening to a lecture. LCT does not do away with lecture, but rather it becomes one of many tools that can help students do the work of learning. As you do more of the work of learning and engage in more regular practice of what you have been asked to learn, long-term potentiation will kick in, and you will start remembering the new learning more easily and for a much longer period, as though you were following a trail already blazed.

Preparing to Learn: Nutrition, Hydration, Sleep, and Exercise

One of the most important new insights into how the human brain learns is that it needs to be prepped for learning if it is to work at its best. Showing up to class without proper sleep and exercise and without eating or hydrating your brain will cause your brain to operate inefficiently and make learning much more difficult.

The human brain uses 25–30% of the body's energy (in the form of glucose) every day (Hallowell, 2005). This means that if you do not have a healthy, balanced diet and eat before you begin new learning, you are starving your brain of the energy it needs to function properly, causing your brain to work much less efficiently. A brain starved for glucose is a brain not ready to learn. The brain does much better if the blood glucose level can be held relatively stable. To do this, avoid simple carbohydrates containing sugar and white flour (e.g., pastries, white bread, and pasta). Rely on the complex carbohydrates found in fruits, whole grains, and vegetables. Protein is important: instead of starting your day with coffee and a donut, try tea and an egg on wheat toast, and take a multivitamin every day (Hallowell, 2005). It is crucial that you eat before you try to learn.

In addition to food, your brain needs a great deal of water. Neurons (brain cells) store water in tiny balloon-like structures called vacuoles. Water is essential for optimal brain health and function. Water is needed for the brain's production of hormones and neurotransmitters. These are the key players in the brain's communication system, which is at the heart of learning (Armstrong et al., 2012). According to Norman (2010), "Dehydration can lead to fatigue, dizziness, poor concentration, and reduced cognitive abilities. Even mild levels of dehydration can impact school performance." When you wake up each morning, you are likely dehydrated. Think about it: you have not had any liquid intake for 6–10 hr, and the body loses a significant amount of water (as much as 2 lb) while it sleeps (Donner, 2011). It is simply not enough to wake up, grab your clothes, and head to class. You need to prepare your brain to learn by hydrating it; otherwise, you are making learning much more difficult for yourself.

Brain research has produced overwhelming evidence of the important role exercise and sleep play in the brain's ability to learn and remember. We see these two areas as so important that we have devoted chapters to each of them. Chapter 2, "Sleep, Naps, and Breaks," covers a wide range of vital information about the relationship of a good night's rest to effective learning and the making of long-term memories, which are the key to college success. Chapter 3, "Exercise and Learning," discusses the profound effect exercise has on improving learning and memory. Exercise may be the most important activity you can take part in to improve your learning.

Preparing the brain to learn is a new idea for most students, but it is crucial to your ability to learn. A tired, hungry, and thirsty brain deprived of the essential benefits exercise brings to it is a brain not ready to learn.

Cramming: "Learning" Without Remembering

You know the outcome of cramming information into your brain only a day or two before a test. Sometimes you make mistakes that you would not have made had you not crammed. These mistakes can be a result of fatigue, of trying to recall information that is not well established, or of confusion among all the material just studied. Sometimes, even if you do remember all the material and get a passing grade on the test, the information is quickly forgotten, and you end up having to relearn it all for the final exam, for a related class the following semester, or for a new job. In fact, the practice of cramming does not meet the neuroscience definition of *learning*, which requires that learned information be available for use at a later time. Permanent memories are formed after distributed practice; cramming, in contrast, typically does not allow the brain to build the strong connection to the new material necessary to establish more permanent memories. So, cramming does not usually result in learning. Learning and remembering material requires work. This work can involve cramming the night before the exam and then completely relearning the material at a later time. Or, it can involve learning it correctly the first time and then having the material available to you later (perhaps at a new job) after a quick review.

Transference of Learning

You can demonstrate learning by using new information to help you learn similar new information or by applying the new information to problems beyond those you have been doing in class. Psychologists call this transference (Barnett & Ceci, 2002). Transference is the principle being tested by the problems on your math exam that are slightly different from those you did in class or were given for homework. The closer the transfer distance, the less you need to understand what you are doing. It is easy to memorize information and then "transfer" it to an almost identical scenario. Real learning happens when you start to increase the distance of the transfer. Your instructor is trying to help you to understand the math by seeing whether you can use the knowledge you have developed to solve new problems.

Life won't give you the exact same problems all the time, and knowing how to apply information to solve new problems is the foundation of being educated. Memorized information might help on a low-level test, but it won't help much in life, unless you get on *Jeopardy!* Look for connections between learned material and new material, and celebrate any time you notice that you have transferred information, particularly when there is a fairly big difference between the problems. Transference of knowledge and skills will help you both ace the final and do well at your future job. That said, learning to transfer new learning is not easy. It typically requires a bit of extra practice. Long-term potentiation helps facilitate transfer. (By the way, if you understand that last sentence, you have already learned a lot and currently know more than most about learning in harmony with your brain.)

Connections With What Has Already Been Learned

The human brain is constantly looking for connections. Connections help you to use prior knowledge to build bridges to new material, creating a more meaningful understanding of the new material. Have you ever noticed how easy it is to remember the name of someone you've just met if he or she looks a bit like a person you know with the same name? If you have played music for a long time, you have seen similar connections in action many times. You likely find it easier to learn a new piece of music if you recognize patterns in it and can connect them to music you already know. Yes, creating connections is also why you had to spend all that time learning musical scales. What is great about how the brain works when learning new material is that the more you learn, the easier it is to learn.

Some subjects are more difficult for you to learn because you lack prior knowledge, not because you lack intelligence. Lack of knowledge makes it difficult for your brain to figure out how to make connections to patterns already known. Everyone accepted into college has the intellectual capabilities necessary to graduate, if he or she is willing to put time and effort into learning. The key to successfully dealing with difficult new material is a willingness to get help filling in missing prior knowledge when you need it and then to practice the new learning enough to make permanent memories. Unfortunately, many students think they are not smart enough to learn difficult material; this indicates that they do not understand how the human brain works. We all get smarter every day by adding to our knowledge and skill base. From there we make new connections that allow us to learn even more. The key to handling difficult subjects is to fill in the background information that you may have not learned in your earlier schooling so that your brain can have something to connect the new knowledge to. If you fill in these knowledge gaps, then your success will depend entirely on the amount of practice you are willing to put in to master a subject. It is true that some people have greater abilities in certain areas, but if you have been accepted into college, you have already demonstrated the abilities necessary to handle the subjects you will be asked to learn. College success does not depend on being smart; it is about learning how to be an effective learner.

The Key Message

The primary message from neuroscience researchers is relatively simple: "The one who does the work does the learning" (Doyle, 2008, p. 63). Only when you practice, read, write, think, talk, collaborate, and reflect does your brain make permanent connections. Your teachers cannot do this for you, and at times this work will make you tired. When you are worn out from learning, rest a bit and reflect on the fact that you are changing the neurochemistry in your brain. That is pretty amazing.

Chapter Summary

There is new understanding about how learning happens, and this new understanding contradicts what most students think happens when they learn. Students need to know the new findings in order to maximize their learning abilities. Following are the key ideas from this chapter:

1. Neuroscience research shows that when you learn something new, there is a physical change in your brain. Some of your brain cells establish connections with other brain cells to form new networks of cells, which represent the new learning that has taken place.
2. Every time you use or practice newly learned information or skills, the connections between the brain cells get stronger and your ability to recall the information becomes faster. This is called long-term potentiation.
3. The important message for all learners is that new learning requires a considerable amount of practice and a meaningful connection to other information in order to become a permanent part of memory.
4. Neuroscience research has also found that to form lasting memories, practice needs to happen over extended periods. Psychologists call this the distributed practice effect.
5. Cramming is not learning. A day or two of cramming is not nearly enough time for the brain to form the permanent memories necessary to meet the neuroscience definition of *learning*.
6. You can demonstrate learning by using new information to help you learn similar new information or by applying it to problems beyond those you have been doing in class. Psychologists call this transference.
7. The human brain is constantly looking for connections to prior knowledge. These connections link previously learned material to new material, creating a more meaningful understanding of the new material.
8. The message from neuroscience researchers is simple: "The one who does the work does the learning" (Doyle, 2008, p. 63). Only when you practice, read, write, think, talk, collaborate, and reflect does your brain make permanent connections. Your teachers cannot do this for you.

References

Anderson, J. R., & Pavlik, P. I. (2008). Using a model to compute the optimal schedule of practice. *Journal of Experimental Psychology: Applied, 14*(2), 101–117.

Armstrong, L., Ganio, M. S., Casa, D. J., Lee, E. C., McDermott, B. P., Klau, J. F., . . . Lieberman, H. R. (2012). Mild dehydration affects mood in healthy young women. *Journal of Nutrition, 142*(2), 382–388. Retrieved from http://jn.nutrition.org/content/early/2011/12/20/jn.111.142000 .abstract

Barnett, S. M., & Ceci, S. J. (2002). When and where do we apply what we learn? A taxonomy for far transfer. *Psychological Bulletin, 128*, 612–637.

Begley, S. (2011, January 3). "Can you build a better brain?" *Newsweek.* Retrieved from http://www.thedailybeast.com/newsweek/2011/01/03/can -you-build-a-better-brain.html

Bibb, J., Mayford, A., Tsien, J., & Alberini, C. (2010, November). Cognition enhancement strategies. *Journal of Neuroscience, 30*(45), 14987–14992. doi:10.1523/JNEUROSCI.4419-1

Donner, E. (2011, June 14). How much weight do you lose during sleep? *Livestrong.com.* Retrieved from http://www.livestrong.com/article/402138 -how-much-weight-do-you-lose-during-sleep/

Doyle, T. (2008). *Helping students learn in a learner-centered environment: A guide to facilitating learning in higher education.* Sterling, VA: Stylus.

Ebbinghaus, H. (1913). *A contribution to experimental psychology.* New York: Teachers College, Columbia University.

Hallowell, E. (2005, January). Overloaded circuits: Why smart people under-perform. *Harvard Business Review.* Retrieved from http://web.mit.edu/mit postdocs/documents/OverloadedCircuits.pdf

Norman, P. (2010). *Feeding the brain for academic success: How nutrition and hydration boost learning.* Retrieved from http://www.healthybrain forlife.com/articles/school-health-and-nutrition/feeding-the-brain-for -academic-success-how

Randerson, J. (2012, February 28). How many neurons make a human brain? Billions fewer than we thought [web post]. *Notes and Theories.* Retrieved from http://www.guardian.co.uk/science/blog/2012/feb/28/

Ratey, J. (2001). *A user's guide to the brain.* New York: Pantheon Books.

2

SLEEP, NAPS, AND BREAKS

How many uninterrupted hours of sleep did you get last night? The night before that? When college students are asked about sleep, most report not getting enough. What has your life looked like over the past week? Are you getting as much sleep as you feel you need? We all know that it is more difficult to learn something new when tired, but the role of sleep and fatigue in learning involves more than having difficulty focusing or staying awake when studying. Human sleep is still not fully understood. There is even debate over why we sleep at all. However, most sleep researchers now agree that sleep plays an important role in the formation of long-term memories (Stickgold, 2005).

The exact relationship between memory formation and sleep is the subject of ongoing research, and new evidence is being discovered all the time (see Box 2.1). We do know, however, that the time, money, and effort you put into learning the content and skills in your courses will be significantly diminished by a lack of sleep. Adults typically need 7.5–9 hr of sleep each night to feel fully rested and function at their best. Yet, Americans are getting less sleep than they did in the past. A 2011 National Sleep Foundation (NSF) poll found that about two thirds (63%) of Americans say their sleep needs are not being met

BOX 2.1
How Neuroscience Findings Change

It was thought for some time that the brain's hippocampus initiated the process that allowed information we wanted to remember to be moved to a more stable area of the brain called the neocortex. Research in 2012 at the University of California–Los Angeles (UCLA) by Mayank Mehta and his colleagues instead showed that the neocortex actually initiates the process. In addition, Mehta found that a part of the brain called the entorhinal cortex plays a significant role in memory formation and involves the hippocampus in memory processing (Mehta, Hahn, McFarland, Berberich, & Sakmann, 2012).

This new finding means that the dialogue among brain areas involved in memory formation is more complex than once thought and that the direction of the communication is the opposite of what was once thought. Memories are still made during sleep, but by a different process.

This example shows that new information about the human brain is discovered all the time, and even the best information we have today may need to be revised as new studies are conducted. All of us as learners will want to pay attention to the new findings.

during the week. Most say they need about 7.5 hr of sleep to feel their best, but they report getting an average of 6 hr and 55 min of sleep on weeknights. About 15% of adults between 19 and 64 years old and 7% of adolescents between 13 and 18 years old say they sleep less than 6 hr on weeknights (NSF, 2011).

What Researchers Say

According to the National Institutes of Health, people 18 years old and older need 7.5–9 hr of sleep each night (Smith, Robinson, & Segal, 2013). Mayank Mehta, a neurophysics professor and memory researcher at the University of California–Los Angeles (UCLA), and his colleagues write, "Humans spend one-third of their lives sleeping, and a lack of sleep results in adverse effects on health, as well as learning and memory problems" (Mehta et al., 2012). Neuroscientist Matthew Walker, director of the Beth Israel Deaconess Medical Center's Sleep and Neuroimaging Laboratory, says, "You can't shortchange your brain of sleep and still learn effectively" (as cited in Beth Israel Deaconess Medical Center, 2005). So, if you are not getting 7.5–9 hr of sleep each night, you are likely sabotaging your own learning.

The Science of Memory and Sleep

György Buzsaki, professor at the Center for Molecular and Behavioral Neuroscience at Rutgers University, and his coresearchers have determined that short transient brain events, called sharp wave ripples, are responsible for consolidating memories and transferring new information from the hippocampus, which is a fast-learning but low-capacity short-term memory store, to the neocortex, which is a slower-learning but higher-capacity long-term memory store (Buzsaki, Girardeau, Benchenane, Wiener, & Zugaro, 2009). Information stored in the neocortex will be more stable and have a greater likelihood, if practiced, of becoming long-term memories (see Figure 2.1). Buzsaki et al. (2009) also found that this movement happens primarily when we are asleep.

Dr. James Maas, presidential fellow and past chair of psychology at Cornell University, indicates in *Sleep for Success*, the book he wrote with Rebecca Robbins, that sleep has a big impact on memory (Maas & Robbins, 2011). Maas writes that a person who is sleep deprived will be 19% less efficient at recalling memories. A person who has not slept at all has 50% less memory ability. Maas goes on to write that the final 2 hr of sleep, from hour 5.5 to 7.5 or hour 7 to 9, are crucial for memories to be laid down as stable residents in your brain. During this period in rapid eye movement (REM) sleep, your brain replays scenes from the day over and over again so that they become stable in your memory (Maas & Robbins, 2011).

Figure 2.1 Sleep helps memory traces to move from the hippocampus to the neocortex, where they are more stable. From www.positscience.com. ©1999 by Scientific Learning Corporation. Reprinted with permission.

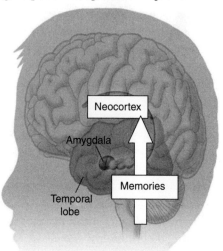

Preparation for the Next Day's Learning

Sleep also serves other functions. In addition to providing opportunity to consolidate learned material, sleep allows your brain to clear space for new learning to occur the next day. University of California–Berkeley (UC Berkeley) researchers have found compelling evidence that during sleep 12- to 14-Hz bursts of brain waves, called sleep spindles, may be networking between key regions of the brain to clear a path for learning (Walker, 2005). These electrical impulses help to shift memories from the brain's hippocampus—which has limited storage space—to the nearly limitless prefrontal cortex's "hard drive," thus freeing up the hippocampus to take in fresh data (new learning).

Matthew Walker says sleep is the key to having a brain that is ready to learn ("Naps Clear the Mind," 2010). Bryce Mander, a postdoctoral fellow in psychology at UC Berkeley and lead author of a study on sleep spindles, adds, "A lot of that spindle-rich sleep is occurring the second half of the night, so if you sleep six hours or less, you are shortchanging yourself and impeding your learning" (as cited in HealthDay News, 2011). Mander goes on to say, "This discovery indicates that we not only need sleep after learning to consolidate what we've memorized, but that we also need it before learning, so that we can recharge and soak up new information the next day" (as cited in HealthDay News, 2011).

Why Sleep Is Crucial to Learning and Memory

Walker says, "When you're asleep, it seems as though you are shifting memories to more efficient storage regions within the brain. Consequently, when you awaken, memory tasks can be performed both more quickly and accurately and with less stress and anxiety" (as cited in Beth Israel Deaconess Medical Center, 2005). Sleep protects new memories from disruption by the interfering experiences that are inevitable during wakefulness (Payne et al., 2012), and during sleep memories are consolidated according to their relative importance, based on your expectations for remembering (Wilhelm et al., 2011). The two key messages here are that, first, new learning is quite fragile and susceptible to change and interference before it is consolidated. REM and slow-wave sleep help to consolidate some memories. Second, according to Payne et al. (2012), "Sleeping soon after learning can benefit both episodic memory (memory for events) and semantic memory (memory for facts about the world)." This means that it would be a good thing to rehearse any information you need to remember immediately before you go to bed. According to Payne et al. (2012), "In some sense, you may be 'telling' the sleeping brain what to consolidate." As learners, you must identify the new learning you want to remember (Payne et al., 2012).

Three Stages of Memory Processing

The three stages of memory processing are encoding, storage, and retrieval. All three are affected in different ways by the amount of sleep you get. It is difficult to encode new learning when you are tired and unable to pay attention to the information. In fact, when you are sleep deprived, it becomes more difficult to learn new information the longer you are awake. Similarly, without the proper amount of sleep, storage of new memories will be disrupted.

The third stage of memory processing is the recall phase (retrieval). During retrieval, the memory is accessed and re-edited. This is often the most important stage, as learned material is of limited value if it can't be recalled when needed, for example, for an exam. Mass and Robbins (2011) write that recall is impeded by a lack of sleep. Converging scientific evidence, from the molecular to the phenomenological, leaves little doubt that memory reprocessing "offline," that is, during sleep (see Box 2.2) is an important component of how our memories are formed, shaped, and remembered (Stickgold, 2005).

BOX 2.2
The Stages of Sleep

Non-REM sleep

Stage N1 (Transition to sleep)—This stage lasts about 5 min. Your eyes move slowly under the eyelids, muscle activity slows down, and you are easily awakened.

Stage N2 (Light sleep)—This is the first stage of true sleep, lasting from 10 to 25 min. Your eye movement stops, heart rate slows, and body temperature decreases.

Stage N3 (Deep sleep)—You're difficult to awaken, and if you are awakened, you do not adjust immediately and often feel groggy and disoriented for several minutes. In this deepest stage of sleep, your brain waves are extremely slow. Blood flow is directed away from your brain and toward your muscles, restoring physical energy.

REM sleep

REM sleep (Dream sleep)—About 70 to 90 min after falling asleep, you enter REM sleep, the stage during which dreaming occurs. Your eyes move rapidly, your breathing becomes shallow, and your heart rate and blood pressure increase. Also during this stage, your arm and leg muscles are paralyzed (Smith et al., 2013).

Larks, Night Owls, and the Rest of Us

Humans differ on many dimensions. Sleep is no exception. Individuals do not need the same amount of sleep. In the absence of alcohol, drugs, or sleep challenges, the most important measure of sleep deprivation is simply how you feel. If you are fatigued, then you need more sleep, even if you regularly sleep 8 hr per night. If you feel rested sleeping 6 hr per night, then that is all the sleep you may need. Individuals also differ on the time of day during which they function at an optimal level. For some, early morning is the best time for serious learning, whereas others best learn later at night. Although no large scientific study of adults has been conducted to confirm that people have defi- nite differences in their sleep patterns, many smaller scientific studies suggest that approximately 20–30% of the adult population is made up of either larks (morning people) or night owls (Monk, 2004; Zee & Turek, 2006).

These variations in sleep patterns, or "chronotypes," are a result of our genes, and although they can change as our lives and work schedules change, the process is not often easy to deal with ("Genes Linked," 2011). Dr. Jim Wilson, author of the University of Edinburgh's Centre for Population Health Sciences study of sleep patterns, found that a tendency to sleep for longer or shorter periods often runs in families, although the amount of sleep people need can also be influenced by age, latitude, season, and circadian rhythms ("Genes Linked," 2011).

If you are most alert around noon each day, do your best work in the hours before you eat lunch, and are ready for bed relatively early each night, you are definitively a morning person, or lark. Knowing you are a lark is important information from the standpoint of learn- ing. Larks are much better off taking classes, doing more challenging homework, and studying during the morning or daytime hours and leaving their easier work until night, when they are likely more tired.

If you are most alert around 6:00 p.m., do your best work late in the evening, and often stay up until 2:00 or 3:00 a.m., you are a night owl. Night owls who take morning classes tend to have more diffi- culty staying awake and paying attention simply because their natural rhythms identify the early morning as a time to sleep. If you are a night owl, sign up for afternoon classes and plan to do challenging home-work and study later in the evening.

If you are a night owl, you should avoid attending 8:00 or 9:00 a.m. classes after only 4–6 hr of sleep. In a 2008 study involving more than 800 students, Dr. Kendry Clay of the University of North Texas found that college students who were evening types (night owls) had lower grade point averages (GPAs) than those who were morning types. One reason for this discrepancy was the great likelihood that the night owls were sleep deprived (American Academy of Sleep Medicine, 2008). In a similar 2012 study at the University of Arkansas on the effects of sleep and anxiety on college students' performance, researchers found that sleep deprivation could lead to a lower GPA (Moran, 2012). Com-menting on that study, Kimberly Fenn, the principal investigator at the Sleep and Learning Lab at Michigan State University, said that although occasionally missing an hour of sleep will not be detrimental to academic performance, students who regularly get only 4 or 5 hr of sleep will most likely have a lower GPA (Moran, 2012). For suggestions for changing your night-owl ways, see Box 2.3.

About 70% of the adult population does not fall into either the lark or night-owl category. If you do not have the tendency to get up very early or stay up very late, you simply need to identify your best time of the day for learning.

Most people have not thought carefully about how to structure their day to optimize their learning time according to natural rhythms. One way to do this is to keep a log for one week. Find or make a chart that starts Sunday night at 6:00 p.m. and has blocks for the 24 hr of each day. Each day when you wake up, fill in the blocks to show the time you slept the night before. Then, periodically through the day, give yourself a grade based on how mentally alert you feel. Your grades will vary greatly based on what you are doing, but over time you will likely see patterns. If you read a chapter of a book and feel like you under-stood it well, give yourself an "A," for alert, during that block of reading time. If you are studying and find yourself losing concentration at times, give yourself an "LC," for losing concentration. If you start to do some homework problems and find yourself getting so distracted that you don't accomplish any work, give yourself a "D," for distracted. These are

---

BOX 2.3
Recommendations for Changing Night-Owl Sleep Patterns

Researchers affiliated with the American Academy of Sleep Medicine suggest that college students reset their internal clocks, a little bit at a time over several weeks, by following these tips:

- Don't pull all-nighters or cram for exams late at night. Instead, do your intense studying in the morning, when your brain is fresh and alert. Schedule study sessions for afternoon.
- Beer and pizza are not good choices close to bedtime. Avoid caffeine, alcohol, heavy exercise, and heavy snacking before bedtime.
- Go to bed at the same time every night—ideally by midnight, so you can get a full night's sleep.
- College kids may consider themselves too old for warm milk and *Goodnight Moon*, but they should make their bedtime routines soothing and consistent. Turn off the cell phone and laptop. Read a book or listen to quiet music.
- Make sure your bedroom is quiet and dark—or if you live in a dorm, invest in a pair of earplugs or noise-cancelling headphones, and a sleep mask.
- Rise at the same time every morning, and get outside. Sunlight helps reset circadian rhythms. (Burrell, 2013)

---

just examples. The idea is to see whether a pattern emerges as to when you concentrate, think, and remember best. You might also see that after a night of almost no sleep, you are "brain dead" most of the next day.

Naps and Wakeful Rest

Did you know that humans are supposed to nap every afternoon? It's true. Dr. William C. Dement, founder of the Stanford University Sleep Clinic and the father of sleep research, found that the human brain experiences transient sleepiness in the midafternoon and that there is nothing we can do about it. In fact, Dement says humans function best with a good night's rest and a short afternoon nap. A person's desire to nap in midafternoon varies in degree, but the fact remains that our brains do not function well when they want to be asleep (Dement & Vaughan, 1999). Psychologist James Maas points out that naps "greatly strengthen the ability to pay close attention to details and to make critical decisions." He adds that "naps taken about eight hours after you wake have been proven to do much more for you than if you added those 20 or 30 min onto your night time sleep" (Maas & Robbins, 2011, p. 33).

One of the dilemmas we all face is that new memories (information just learned) are stored temporarily in a region of the brain called the hippocampus. While in this area, newly learned information is fragile and can be easily changed or forgotten. The information needs to be transferred to more permanent storage areas in the brain or else it is susceptible to being replaced by other new learning. Dr. Michaela Dewar and her colleagues, in a study published in *Psychological Science*, found that memory can be boosted by taking a brief wakeful rest after learning something verbally new (Dewar, Alber, Butler, Cowan, & Della Sala, 2012). The findings of Dewar et al. (2012) suggest that the point at which we experience new information is "just at a very early stage of memory formation and that further neural processes have to occur after this stage for us to be able to remember this information at a later point in time" (p. 35). The authors went on to say that

> researchers believe the new input crowds out recently acquired information, indeed, our work demonstrates that activities that we are engaged in for the first few minutes after learning new information really affect how well we remember this information after a week. (Dewar et al., 2012)

Dewar et al. (2012) demonstrate that activities that we are engaged in for the first few minutes after learning new information affect how well we remember this information. These findings suggest that students should engage in periods of wakeful rest, including daydreaming and thinking, following new learning. The key aspects of this pause are to keep the eyes closed and to not be distracted or receive new information (Dewar et al., 2012).

The findings of Dewar et al. (2012) suggest, from a learning perspective, that taking classes back-to-back may not be a great idea. Back-to-back class schedules may cut down on travel time to and from campus and allow for better work schedules, but they leave no time for consolidation in the brain of the material presented during the first class.

Another excellent way to consolidate memories, especially if you have afternoon classes, is to take a brief nap of 20–30 min. During this short nap, new learning becomes more stable. Thus, it will more likely be available in its original form when you go to practice it in the future.

Researchers at the University of Lübeck in Germany conducted a study that demonstrated that students who napped after learning 15 pairs of cards with animals on them remembered 85% of the cards, whereas students who learned the same cards but did not nap recalled only 60% (Diekelmann, Büchel, Born, & Rasch, 2011). In another nap study, the National Aeronautics and Space Administration (NASA) found that pilots who took a 26-min nap increased their flying performance by 34% over their performances when no rest was taken. NASA also discovered that a 45-min nap gave astronauts a boost in their cognitive (thinking) performance for 6 hr following the nap (NASA, 2005).

Remembering What Is Important During Sleep

Sleep is important but not equally important for all information. According to a study published in the *Journal of Neuroscience* by Dr. Ines Wilhelm and her colleagues (2011), people remember information better after a good night's sleep when they know it will be useful in the future. This finding suggests that the brain evaluates memories during sleep and preferentially retains those that are most likely to be important and needed relatively soon (Wilhelm et al., 2011). The study also found that the students who slept right after learning new material and who knew they were going to be tested on that material had substantially improved memory recall over students who knew they would not be tested on the newly learned material. The authors suggest that the brain's prefrontal cortex "tags" memories deemed relevant while awake and that the hippocampus consolidates these memories during sleep (Wilhelm et al., 2011).

Sleep Deprivation and Learning

If you are between the ages of 18 and 25, you are part of a generation that seems to love stimulating the brain with multiple and constant sensory inputs. Whether it is listening to music, texting, phoning, watching TV, or playing video games, you are engaging in activities that can exhaust your brain and impede learning, and you may not even be aware that your brain is tired (Berman, Jonides, & Kaplan, 2008). The brain was not built for constant sensory stimulation.

Constantly taxing your brain is not the only way to exhaust it. Another common cause of brain exhaustion is sleep deprivation. One of the most significant findings from sleep researchers is the profound effect getting too little sleep has on learning and memory. A recent University of Cincinnati study showed that only 24% of college students report that they are getting adequate sleep, and a Brown University study showed that only 11% of college students are getting enough sleep (Peek, 2012). Researchers at the University of California–San Francisco discovered that some people have a gene that enables them to do well on 6 hr of sleep a night. But the gene is rare and appears in less than 3% of the population. For the other 97% of us, 6 hr doesn't come close to cutting it (He et al., 2009).

A sleep debt is the difference between the amount of sleep a person should be getting and the amount he or she actually gets. It's a deficit that grows every time we skim some extra minutes off our nightly slumber. Dement and Vaughan (1999) say that people accumulate sleep debt without realizing it and that operating with a sleep debt is bad for learning. The short-term effects of sleep deprivation include a foggy brain, worsened vision, impaired driving, and trouble remembering. Long-term effects include obesity, insulin resistance, and heart disease.

Unfortunately, we are not good at perceiving the detrimental effects of sleep deprivation. Researchers at the University of Pennsylvania restricted volunteers to less than 6 hr in bed per night for two weeks. The volunteers perceived only a small increase in sleepiness and thought they were functioning relatively normally. However, formal testing showed that their cognitive abilities and reaction times progressively declined during the two weeks. By the end of the two-week test, they were as impaired as subjects who had been awake continuously for 48 hr (Van Dongen, Maislin, Mullington, & Dinges, 2003).

In a 2012 study, UCLA professor of psychiatry Andrew J. Fuligni and his colleagues reported that sacrificing sleep for extra study time, whether it's cramming for a test or plowing through a pile of homework, is actually counterproductive. Regardless of how much a student studies each day on average, if that student sacrifices sleep time in order to study more than usual, he or she is likely to have more academic problems, not fewer, the following day ("Cramming," 2012).

Sleeping and Diet

In a 2013 study, Dr. Michael Grandner and his colleagues from the University of Pennsylvania Center for Sleep and Circadian Neurobiology found that people who have a healthy diet and eat a large variety of foods have the healthiest sleep patterns (Lynn, 2013). Numerous studies link sleep deprivation with obesity, so it may not be surprising that a healthy diet is a major predictor of good sleep habits.

Fixing a Sleep Debt

Recovering from one or two nights' sleep deprivation is accomplished by getting a good night's rest. Just one night of recovery sleep can reverse the adverse effects of total sleep deprivation. Recovery sleep is more efficient than normal sleep. Most people fall asleep faster than normal and have increased amounts of deep and REM sleep. A good practice is to sleep until you wake up on your own—don't set an alarm.

Recovering from a longer period of sleep deprivation can be trickier. First, you must realize that you are the one who decides how much sleep you get, as you manage the demands on yourself and your time. College allows for many opportunities, but each opportunity comes with a cost of time. For those who have so many obligations that they sleep less than typically recommended and are coping with a long-term sleep debt, the American Academy of Sleep Medicine recommends the following short-term solutions for reducing the effects of sleep deprivation. Note, however, that following these suggestions may not restore alertness and performance to fully rested levels (Widmar, 2003).

- Caffeine: Caffeine is arguably the most commonly ingested stimulant, as it is used regularly by 80% of adults in the United States in liquid, tablet, or gum form. It can provide improved alertness and performance at doses of 75 mg to 150 mg after acute sleep loss. Higher doses are required to produce a benefit after a night or more of total sleep loss. A person who uses caffeine frequently can build up a tolerance to the substance, which makes it less and less effective.
- Naps: During a period of sleep loss, a brief nap of 30 min or less may boost alertness. Be cautious of longer naps, however, because they can be difficult to wake up from and they may also produce severe grogginess, or "sleep inertia," that persists after waking up.
- Caffeine and a nap: The beneficial effects of a nap taken when experiencing sleep deprivation combined with the use of caffeine following the nap may be additive. Combining a nap with caffeine use during sleep deprivation can provide improved alertness over a longer period.
- A doctor visit: Talk to your doctor about why you are failing to get adequate sleep and ask for recommendations for coping with the sleep debt.

Staying Out of Sleep Debt

The following are some additional tips for getting and staying out of sleep debt (Smith et al., 2013):

- Schedule time for sleep and aim for at least 7.5 hr of sleep every night. Block off enough time for sleep each night so that you don't fall further in debt. Consistency is the key.
- Settle short-term sleep debt as soon as possible. Recovery sleep can get you back to optimum learning levels.
- Keep a sleep diary. Record when you go to bed, when you get up, your total hours of sleep, and how you feel during the day. As you keep track of your sleep, you'll discover your natural patterns and get to know your sleep needs.

How to Avoid a Sleep Debt

To avoid falling into a sleep-debt situation, it is important to know how to get a good night's rest. It sounds silly to offer advice on how to do something that is a natural process for all humans, and yet numerous studies indicate that most students don't get enough sleep and that the sleep they do get is not as restful as it needs to be. Following are a few ways to get the quality sleep you need (Smith et al., 2013):

- Pay attention to what you eat and drink. Don't go to bed either hungry or stuffed. Your discomfort might keep you up.
- Be careful when using nicotine, caffeine, and alcohol. The stimulating effects of nicotine and caffeine, which take hours to wear off, can wreak havoc on quality sleep. And even though alcohol might make you feel sleepy, it actually disrupts sleep later in the night.
- Create a bedtime ritual. Do the same things each night to tell your body it's time to wind down. This might include taking a warm bath or shower, reading a book, or listening to soothing music with the lights dimmed.
- Get comfortable. Create a room that's ideal for sleeping. Often this means cool, dark, and quiet.
- Limit daytime naps. Long daytime naps can interfere with nighttime sleep especially if you're struggling with insomnia or poor sleep quality at night. Naps can be very positive but should

be limited to one nap of 10–30 min, ideally taken during the midafternoon.

- Include physical activity in your daily routine. Regular physical activity can promote better sleep, helping you to fall asleep faster and to enjoy deeper sleep. However, if you exercise too close to bedtime, you might be too energized to fall asleep.

- Stick to a sleep schedule. Go to bed at the same time every day, even on weekends, holidays, and days off. Being consistent reinforces your body's sleep-wake cycle. There's a caveat, though. If you don't fall asleep within about 15 min, get up and do something relaxing. Go back to bed when you're tired.

- Manage stress. If you are lying in bed and your mind is racing through all you have to do the next day (a common occurrence when under stress), your sleep is likely to suffer. To help restore peace to your life, consider healthy ways to manage stress. Start with the basics, such as getting organized, setting priorities, and delegating tasks. Give yourself permission to take a break when you need one.

- Know when to contact your doctor. Nearly everyone has an occasional sleepless night, but if you frequently have trouble sleeping, or if you are very concerned about your lack of sleep, contact your doctor.

- Listen to Marconi Union's song "Weightless." In the 2011 invention issue of *Time* magazine, the song "Weightless," which lasts 8 min and 10 s, was listed as a breakthrough in helping people fall asleep. A listener's body rhythms will sync with the song, slowing heart rate by 35% and reducing anxiety by 65%. Scientists believe that this song works so well that they actually recommend not listening to it while driving.

Chapter Summary

Sleep is so vital to the human body and brain that a continued lack of it can lead to severe illnesses. Many people know this is true and would never try to stay awake for days at a time. What many students do not know is that a full night's sleep every night is vital to learning and memory formation. During sleep humans make memories and the human brain clears away unwanted information so that it will be ready to learn the next day. When you are sleep deprived, you impair your ability to pay attention and learn new information, and your brain has trouble making memories for information that you need to remember, such as your course work. Following are the key ideas from this chapter:

1. Memories are made during sleep.
2. Almost every person needs 7.5–9 hr of sleep each night, and teenagers often need even more.
3. Sleep is when the brain clears the hippocampus of unwanted information so that it is ready to learn new information the next day.
4. Each person has his or her own sleep pattern. Some are morning people, some are night owls, and some fall in between. It is important to find your sleep pattern.
5. The brain remembers best what is most important to you, and recalling the most important information right before bed improves memory formation for that information.
6. A daily 20- to 30-min nap is great for improving learning and memory.
7. Constant sensory stimulation of your brain (e.g., listening to music hour after hour or constantly texting) can exhaust the brain and make learning difficult.
8. Sleep deprivation is harmful to learning and memory.
9. If you have significant sleep problems, get help immediately. Sleep is vital to college success.

References

American Academy of Sleep Medicine. (2008, May 15). Morningness a predictor of better grades in college [News release]. Retrieved from http://www.aasmnet.org/articles.aspx?id=887

Berman, M., Jonides, J., & Kaplan, S. (2008, December). The cognitive benefits of interacting with nature. *Psychological Science, 19*, 1207–1212.

Beth Israel Deaconess Medical Center. (2005, June 29). Study shows how sleep improves memory. *Science Daily.* Retrieved from http://www.sciencedaily .com/releases/2005/06/050629070337.htm

Burrell, J. (2013). College kids, sleep and the GPA connection. *About.com Young Adults.* Retrieved from http://youngadults.about.com/od/healthandsafety/a/ Sleep.htm

Buzsaki, G., Girardeau, G., Benchenane, K., Wiener, S., & Zugaro, M. (2009). Selective suppression of hippocampal ripples impairs spatial memory. *Nature Neuroscience, 12,* 1222–1223. doi:10.1038/nn.2384

Cramming for a test? Don't do it, say UCLA researchers. (2012, August 22). *UC Health.* Retrieved from http://health.universityofcalifornia.edu/ 2012/08/22/cramming-for-a-test-dont-do-it-say-ucla-researchers/

Dement, W. C., & Vaughan, H. C. (1999). *The promise of sleep.* New York: Delacourt Press.

Dewar, M., Alber, J., Butler, C., Cowan, N., & Della Sala, S. (2012, September). Brief wakeful resting boosts new memories over the long term. *Psychological Science, 23*(9), 955–960. doi:10.1177/0956797612441220

Diekelmann, S., Büchel, C., Born, J., & Rasch, B. (2011, January 23). Labile or stable: Opposing consequences for memory when reactivated during wakefulness and sleep. *Nature Neuroscience.* doi:10.1038/nn.2744

Genes linked to need for sleep. (2011). *TheFamilyGP.com.* Retrieved from http://www.thefamilygp.com/Genes-linked-to-needing-more-sleep.htm

He, Y., Jones, C. R., Fujiki, N., Xu, Y., Guo, B., Holder, J., . . . Fu, Y. (2009, August). The transcriptional repressor DEC2 regulates sleep length in mammals. *Science, 325*(5942), 866–870. doi:10.1126/science.1174443

HealthDay News. (2011, March 8). *Brain's learning ability seems to recharge during light slumber.* Retrieved from http://www.alegentcreighton.com/ body.cfm?id=4794&action=detail&ref=50872

Lynn, J. (2013, February 8). New Penn study links eating, sleeping habits. *Newsworks.* Retrieved from http://www.newsworks.org/index.php/local// healthscience/50754

Maas, J., & Robbins, R. (2011). *Sleep for success.* Bloomington, IN: Authorhouse.

Mehta, M., Hahn, T., McFarland, J., Berberich, S., & Sakmann, B. (2012). Spontaneous persistent activity in entorhinal cortex modulates cortico-hippocampal interaction in vivo. *Nature Neuroscience, 15,* 1531–1538. doi:10.1038/nn.3236

Monk, T. (2004, May). Morningness-eveningness and lifestyle regularity. *Chronobiology International, 21*(3), 435–443.

Moran, D. (2012, September 18). Study shows relationship between sleep and GPA. *State News*. Retrieved from http://statenews.com/index.php/article/2012/09/study_shows_relationship_between_sleep_and_gpa

Naps clear the mind, help you learn. (2010, February 21). *Live Science*. Retrieved from http://www.livescience.com/9819-naps-clear-mind-learn.html

National Aeronautics and Space Administration (NASA). (2005, June 3). *NASA nap study*. http://science.nasa.gov/science-news/science-at-nasa/2005/03jun_naps/

National Sleep Foundation (NSF). (2011, March 7). *Annual sleep in America poll exploring connections with communications technology use and sleep*. Retrieved from http://www.sleepfoundation.org/article/press-release/annual-sleep-america-poll-exploring-connections-communications-technology-use-

Payne, J. D., Tucker, M. A., Ellenbogen, J. M., Wamsley, E. J., Walker, M. P., Schacter, D. L., & Stickgold, R. (2012). Memory for semantically related and unrelated declarative information: The benefit of sleep, the cost of wake. *PLoS ONE, 7*(3), e33079. doi:10.1371/journal.pone.0033079

Peek, H. (2012, October 25). Abnormal sleep patterns lead to greater issues. *Tulane Hullabaloo*. Retrieved from http://www.thehullabaloo.com/views/article_2825a6ac-1ee4-11e2-ad21-001a4bcf6878.html

Smith, M., Robinson, L., & Segal, R. (2013, January). How much sleep do you need? Sleep cycles & stages, lack of sleep, and how to get the hours you need. *HelpGuide.org*. Retrieved from http://www.helpguide.org/life/sleeping.htm

Stickgold, R. (2005, October 27). Sleep-dependent memory consolidation. *Nature, 437*, 1272–1278. doi:10.1038/nature04286

Van Dongen, H., Maislin, G., Mullington, J., & Dinges, D. (2003). The cumulative cost of additional wakefulness: Dose-response effects on neurobehavioral functions and sleep physiology from chronic sleep restriction and total sleep deprivation. *Sleep, 26*(2), 117–126. Retrieved from http://www.med.upenn.edu/uep/user_documents/dfd16.pdf

Walker, M. (2005). A refined model of sleep and the time course of memory formation. *Behavioral and Brain Science, 28*, 51–104.

Widmar, R. (2003, June 1). Sleep to survive: How to manage sleep deprivation. *Fire Engineering*. Retrieved from http://www.fireengineering.com/articles/print/volume-156/issue-6/features/sleep-to-survive-how-to-manage-sleep-deprivation.html

Wilhelm, I., Diekelmann, S., Molzow, I., Ayoub, A., Molle, M., & Born, J. (2011). Sleep selectively enhances memory expected to be of future relevance. *Neuroscience, 31*(5), 1563. doi:10.1523/JNEUROSCI.3575-10

Zee, P., & Turek, F. (2006, September). Sleep and health: Everywhere and in both directions. *Journal Archives of Internal Medicine, 166,* 1686–1688.

3

EXERCISE AND LEARNING

One of the most important discoveries about how the human brain learns pertains to an area that few expect. Most people think practice and effort are the two most important aspects of learning. These factors are very important, but recently, research has revealed that having your brain ready to learn also plays a significant role in the process. Getting adequate exercise, especially aerobic exercise, is "the single most important thing a person can do to improve their learning" (Ratey, 2008). Harvard psychiatrist and author John Ratey has written an entire book about how profoundly exercise impacts human learning. The book, *Spark: The Revolutionary New Science of Exercise and the Brain*, reveals that when humans exercise, specific neurochemicals and proteins—messengers of the brain—are released in greater amounts. These chemicals and proteins improve human ability to take in, process, and remember new information and skills. This chapter will introduce you to some of the science behind exercise and suggest ways to integrate it into your college life.

Movement and the Evolution of the Human Brain

The first animals to have a nervous system and potential for movement had a tremendous advantage over, for example, sponges, which had to wait brainlessly for dinner to arrive (Franklin Institute, 2004). Although a great deal of our evolutionary history remains clouded in controversy, one thing paleoanthropologists agree on is that humans were continually on the move. Anthropologist Richard Wrangham says a few hundred thousand years ago, men moved about 10–20 km a day and women moved about half that a day. The human brain developed while in almost constant motion (Medina, 2008). Unfortunately, modern conveniences have made it possible to interact within our communities with very little movement. It turns out that this may not be helpful when it comes to learning.

The Disadvantages of Sitting at Your Desk

An abundance of evidence supports the importance of exercise in students' ability to learn (Ratey, 2008; Reilly, Buskist, & Gross, 2012). Our brains were shaped and sharpened by movement. We continue to require regular physical activity in order for our brains to function optimally (Raichlen & Polk, 2013). Being in motion, by walking, for example, when thinking about how to solve a problem, developing ideas for a paper, brainstorming a great speech, or performing many other learning tasks is an optimal way to learn (Ratey, 2008). (Note, however, that although aerobics plays a significant role in improving learning, as will be explained later in this chapter, trying to learn new or difficult material while engaged in aerobics is counterproductive, as blood flows away from the brain during aerobics.) In some significant ways schools have had it wrong for 200 years. Whereas sitting at desks is practical for taking notes, it is not nearly as effective as walking when learning new material.

Research on Movement and Learning

Flash forward from 200,000 years ago to 1995. In that year Carl Cotman, director of the Institute for Brain Aging and Dementia at the University of California–Irvine, discovered that exercise sparks the master molecule of the learning process: brain-derived neurotrophic factor (BDNF; Cotman, Berchtold, & Christie, 2007). BDNF is a protein produced inside nerve cells when they are active. It serves as fertilizer for brain cells, keeping them functioning and growing, as well as spurring the growth of new neurons. BDNF makes learning easier. With this discovery, Cotman demonstrated a direct biological connection between movement and learning. Since Cotman's finding, thousands of studies on BDNF have shown its power to improve learning.

Ratey (2008) writes, "Exercise strengthens the cellular machinery of learning [by creating BDNF, which] gives the synapses the tools they need to take in information, process it, associate it, remember it, and put it in context" (p. 45). BDNF improves every aspect of the learning process at the cellular level. Ratey (2008) calls it "Miracle-Gro for the Brain." Research by UCLA neuroscientist Fernando Gómez-Pinilla and his colleagues shows that a brain low on BDNF shuts itself off to new information (Ying, Vaynman, & Gómez-Pinilla, 2004).

Brain-Derived Neurotrophic Factor

When the protein BDNF is present in your brain in greater amounts, your brain is better able to make the connections between the brain cells (neural networks) that are the physical representation of what you have learned. To reiterate: this protein actually makes learning easier. The last statement is so important that I am going to say it again—BDNF produced by exercise makes learning easier. This protein gathers in reserve pools near synapses in the brain and is unleashed when we get our blood pumping. BDNF also works to limit the impact of stress on the brain and protect the brain from some diseases (Oregon Health and Science University, 2003). A lack of BDNF makes it harder to learn what you need to know.

Production of Vital Neurochemicals

Exercise increases the production of three important neurochemicals that are involved in learning: serotonin, dopamine, and norepineph-rine. These neurochemicals help your brain to be alert, attentive, motivated for learning, and positive toward learning (because of an improved mood). They also help to enhance our patience and self-control. All these conditions are crucial to successful learning (Ratey, 2008), but as you know, staying awake, focused, motivated, and positive on a daily basis can be difficult in college. If you are alert, focused, attentive, positive, motivated, and engaged in the learning activities of the class, you likely have found the perfect way to learn. By increasing your levels of these three neurochemicals, exercise gives you the tools you need to make any learning situation highly productive.

Growing New Synapses

Synapses are structures that permit a neuron (brain cell) to pass an electrical or chemical signal to another cell, allowing the cells to combine in networks. In this manner cells communicate with one another. Exercise prepares and encourages nerve cells to bind to one another, and this binding is the cellular basis for learning new information. Exercise stimulates the production of new synapses. This is significant because the number of synapses and their efficiency underlie superior intelligence (Kramer et al., 2010). Or, put simply, exercise makes it easier for you to grow smarter.

One piece of evidence that supports this finding comes from a 1999 study done in Naperville Public Schools in Illinois, where aerobic exercise was added to the junior high school curriculum. Results show significant increases in students' test scores even for tests on which U.S. schools often rank well below their world counterparts, such as the Trends in International Mathematics and Science Study (TIMSS) test. The eighth-grade students in Naperville finished first in the world in science, just ahead of Singapore, and sixth in math, trailing only Singapore, South Korea, Taiwan, Hong Kong, and Japan (Ratey, 2008, p. 14).

Yes, these were middle-class youngsters from a good school system, but in the years before the exercise requirement was added, the Naperville schools did not match neighboring schools in per-pupil funding or ACT average score. There was nothing to suggest that this kind of accomplishment was in the Naperville students' future. Only 7% of U.S. students even score in the top tier of TIMSS.

An additional positive, albeit unexpected, finding from the study was the 66% decline in behavior problems and suspensions following the introduction of aerobic activities at the school. This improvement in behavior was correlated with the additional serotonin, dopamine, and norepinephrine—which have been shown to improve mood, motivation, and concentration in learners—in the students' brains.

Growing New Brain Cells

Exercise also spurs the development of new brain cells. These cells develop as stem cells and form in the hippocampus, an important memory area of the brain. The relationship between growing new brain cells and improved learning continues to be studied, but there are indications that growing more brain cells helps improve learning and memory. In a 2007 study, Columbia University Medical Center neurologist Scott Small and Salk Institute neurobiologist Fred Gage found that the new neurons created by exercise cropped up in only one place: the dentate gyrus of the hippocampus, an area that controls learning and memory (Ratey, 2008). The study found that exercise seems to restore the dentate gyrus of the hippocampus to a healthier, "younger" state. Although evidence suggests there is less neurogenesis (i.e., new brain cell growth) as we age, exercise has been shown to be powerful in keeping brain functions healthy and productive at all ages (Ratey, 2008).

What Happens in Your Brain When You Exercise

It is important to mention that any movement is better than no movement when it comes to improving learning. However, the real benefit that neuroscience researchers have discovered comes from regular physical activity or exercise and, in particular, aerobic exercise. Aerobic exercise is an activity that raises the body's demand for oxygen, resulting in a temporary increase in respiration rate and heart rate. Your heart becomes stronger and works more efficiently with regular aerobic exercise. But be sure to check with your doctor before you start a new exercise program.

Many in the exercise field suggest that to do aerobic exercise effectively, you need to get your heart rate beating at 60–70% of its capacity. The appropriate heart-rate level is different for everyone. A list of target heart rates by age is presented in Table 3.1. Someone new to aerobics should start with a target heart rate of 50% of his or her maximum heart rate ("Heart Rate Chart," 2009). If you are a 20-year-old female, your initial 50% target heart rate would be 103 beats per minute (bpm); if you are a 20-year-old male, it would be 100 bpm ("Heart Rate Chart," 2009). Knowing your target heart rate can help you pace yourself during aerobic exercise sessions.

TABLE 3.1 Target Heart Rate During Exercise	
Age	**Min–Max Heart Rate (bpm)**
15	123–164
20	120–160
25	117–156
30	114–152
35	111–148
40	108–144
45	105–140
50	102–136
55	99–132
60	96–128
65	90–120
70	90–120
75	87–116

Note: From Heart rate chart. (2009). *Heart.com*. www.heart.com/heart-rate-chart.html

Aerobic exercise can be any activity that uses large muscles in continuous rhythmic motion to elevate your heart rate (e.g., jogging, bicycling, rowing). The American Heart Association (AHA) recommends aerobic activity for at least 30 min on most days of the week. According to AHA, your target heart rate should be 50% of your maximum heart rate for the first few weeks. You can build up to 75% gradually over a six-month period and then up to 85%. These are target values. You don't have to exercise that hard to stay in shape. For the sake of learning and health, you just need to have aerobic exercise in your life (Mayo Clinic, 2011).

How Much Exercise Is Needed

The question of how much exercise is needed to experience learning benefits has not been fully answered. It is clear, however, that trying to learn something that is new, difficult, or complex while engaged in aerobic activity is a bad idea. When engaged in aerobic activity, blood flows away from the prefrontal cortex (the chief executive officer of our brains) and hampers learning (Ratey, 2008). However, once your exercise is completed, blood flow returns to the prefrontal cortex almost immediately, creating an ideal time for learning to take place.

Ratey (2008) suggests that 30 min of exercise in which our heart rates reach the appropriate levels for our age, four to five times a week, is a good baseline. He also points out that the learning benefits of exercise last for 6–8 hr following activity, and a regular routine of aerobic exercise four to five times a week has significant long-term benefits for learners (Ratey, 2008). An exercise regimen puts your brain in a state of continual readiness to learn. Remember that any exercise is beneficial, but aerobic exercise is the gold standard.

Balance Balls and Mini Stationary Bikes

There are many ways to add exercise to your life, even if you can't get to a gym every day. Many schools across the country allow students to sit on balance balls instead of chairs. A balance ball gives the learner greater freedom of movement, including the ability to bounce up and down at will. This small amount of movement has been shown to keep the prefrontal cortex more engaged (Kilbourne, 2009) and to help with paying attention, which is a critical first step to learning anything.

I was recently on a college campus in Houston where, to my surprise, in the student computer lab under every computer was a mini stationary bike. Students could sit at a computer and pedal away for miles while writing their papers or doing their homework.

There are many ways to add more movement to your learning. Some furniture companies make treadmill desks that allow for computer work, reading, and writing to be done while walking at 0.5–1 mph.

Walking to Class

One of the simplest ways to add exercise to your life is to walk to class, during breaks from study, or after class. If you strapped on a pedometer, you would be surprised how many steps you take each day crisscrossing the campus. Stay out of elevators. Also, park farther away from campus or on the far side of the parking lot (provided the area is safe for walking); this is not only good for your brain but also has the additional benefit of reducing dings in your car doors.

Chapter Summary

This chapter discussed new research findings that clearly show how exercise leads to improved learning and memory. It shared how the release of certain neurochemicals and proteins during exercise, especially aerobic exercise, can cause the brain to be better prepared and able to learn. The chapter also showed that humans are supposed to move when learning and that almost all movement is good for learning. (Note, however, that although aerobics plays a significant role in improving learning, trying to learn new or difficult material while engaged in aerobics is counterproductive.) Following are the key ideas from this chapter:

1. Getting exercise is the best thing you can do to improve your learning.
2. Aerobic exercise, 30 min a day, four to five days a week, is the gold standard for improving learning.
3. All movement is good for learning. Walking to class, sitting on a balance ball instead of a chair, or pedaling a mini stationary bike while studying all help learning.
4. BDNF is a protein that is released during exercise and that makes it easier for the brain to learn. BDNF has been called "Miracle-Gro for the Brain."
5. The neurochemicals serotonin, dopamine, and norepinephrine, which are released in greater amounts during exercise, improve your ability to pay attention, focus, and concentrate. They also improve motivation, mood, and self-discipline.
6. Memory is also helped by exercise.

References

Cotman, C., Berchtold, W., & Christie, L. A. (2007). Corrigendum: Exercise builds brain health: Key roles of growth factor cascades and inflammation. *Trends in Neurosciences, 30*(10), 489.

Franklin Institute. (2004). Renew—Exercise. *The Human Brain.* Retrieved from http://www.fi.edu/learn/brain/exercise.html

Heart rate chart. (2009). *Heart.com.* Retrieved from http://www.heart.com/heart-rate-chart.html

Kilbourne, J. (2009). Sharpening the mind through movement: Using exercise balls as chairs in a university class. *Chronicle of Kinesiology and Physical Education in Higher Education, 20*(1), 10–15. Retrieved from http://www.nakpehe.org/publications/Chronicle%20Issues/ChronicleFebruary2009.pdf

Kramer, A. F., Voss, M. W., Ericjson, K. I., Prakash, R. S., Chaddock, L., Malkowski, E., . . . McAuley, E. (2010). Functional connectivity: A source of variance in the association between cardiorespiratory fitness and cognition? *Neuropsychologia, 48,* 13943–1406.

Mayo Clinic. (2011, February 12). Aerobic exercise: Top 10 reasons to get physical. Retrieved from http://www.mayoclinic.com/health/aerobic-exercise/EP00002

Medina, J. (2008). *Brain rules.* Seattle, WA: Pear Press.

Oregon Health and Science University. (2003, September 29). "Good" chemical: Neurons in brain elevated among exercise addicts. *ScienceDaily.* Retrieved from http://www.sciencedaily.com/releases/2003/09/030929053719.htm

Raichlen, D. A., & Polk, J. D. (2013, January 7). Linking brains and brawn: Exercise and the evolution of human neurobiology. *Proceedings of the Royal Society B: Biological Sciences, 280*(1750). doi:10.1098/rspb.2012.2250

Ratey, J. (2008). *Spark: The revolutionary new science of exercise and the brain.* New York: Little, Brown.

Reilly, E., Buskist, C., & Gross, M. K. (2012). Movement in the classroom: Boosting brain power, fighting obesity. *Kappa Delta Pi Record, 48*(2), 62–66. doi:10.1080/00228958.2012.680365

Ying, Z., Vaynman, S., & Gómez-Pinilla, F. (2004). Exercise induces BDNF and synapses to specific hippocampal subfields. *Journal of Neuroscientific Research, 76*(3), 356–362.

4

USING ALL YOUR SENSES TO LEARN

New Findings About Human Senses

Not long ago most scientists who studied the human senses believed that each sense operated independently. As has been the case with many beliefs about the human brain, new research demonstrates that this belief was in error. New findings show clearly that the human senses work in cooperation with each other and that when two or more senses are used together, learning and memory get a boost. Ladan Shams and Aaron R. Seitz, in their 2008 article "Benefits of Multisensory Learning," write,

> It is likely that the human brain has evolved to develop, learn and operate optimally in multisensory environments. We suggest that training protocols that employ unisensory stimulus regimes (e.g., lectures) do not engage multisensory learning mechanisms and, therefore, might not be optimal for learning. However, multisensory-training protocols can better approximate natural settings and are more effective for learning. (Shams & Seitz, 2008, p. 411)

Put simply, a multisensory approach to learning is much better than a unisensory one.

Even before there was scientific proof that the senses work together, researchers were testing the use of multiple senses in learning. In studies conducted as early as 1969, it was demonstrated that students who used both their auditory (hearing) and visual (seeing) senses remembered 20–40% more information after two weeks than students who either listened to or read the information (Dale, 1969).

Each of our senses provides additional retrieval cues for information and builds a more complete experience of a concept or an idea. Because multisensory learning gives you more than one way of experiencing something, it's an ideal way to learn. John Medina, author of the book *Brain Rules*, writes, "[Those] in multisensory environments always do better than [those] in unisensory environments. . . . Their recall has better resolution and lasts longer, evident even 20 *years* later" (Medina, 2008, p. 208; italics in original). Box 4.1 provides an example of multisensory learning.

BOX 4.1
Learning Using Multiple Senses

During the spring semester, I teach a course for students who have ended up on academic probation. I call the class "I Should Have Studied Smarter 100." One thing I want my students to understand is how nutrition affects learning. To enhance recall on this topic, I use a multisensory approach to discuss the amount of sugar and fat in cola and fast-food hamburgers—favorites of many college students.

My tools include a full sugar bowl, a few teaspoons, shortening, and two clear 8-oz glasses. I begin by filling a glass with sugar 1 tsp at a time, asking the students to stop me when they think I have put the amount of sugar in a 20-oz cola in the glass. Without fail, they stop me several times before I get to 17 tsp. I hold up the glass so that my students can see how much sugar they take in when they drink 20-oz of cola. The 8-oz glass is nearly one third full. I don't stop with just this visual display (Sensory Process 1: Vision).

I then pass the glass around the room for students to take a close look at the amount of sugar and to feel its weight (Sensory Process 2: Touch). When the glass is returned to me, I take a teaspoon, fill it with sugar, stick it in my mouth, and swallow it (Sensory Process 3: Taste). Students actually cringe at seeing me do this. I then take another spoon and ask for volunteers to eat a spoonful of sugar. I want my students to taste the sugar. I can usually get a few helpful volunteers to try it. I point out that we ate only one spoonful and everyone was cringing, yet we will drink 17 tsp over lunch with little thought or concern.

Next, I take out a can of shortening and begin filling another 8-oz glass with shortening. This time I ask them to tell me when they think I have put the amount of fat in a single fast-food hamburger, 53 g (53 g = 0.11699 lb). After arriving at the 53 g, I repeat the same process of passing the glass around the class so that students can feel the weight. When the glass is returned to me, I take out another spoon, fill it with the shortening, and eat it. Absolute horror appears on my students' faces. No one is willing to follow my lead and eat a spoonful.

Every semester this multisensory lesson on nutrition is identified by most students as what they remember best from the class.

Multisensory Research Findings

In a 2008 study Shams and Seitz found that multisensory learning is essential to increasing the probability that the human brain will retain information from a particular event. Their research found that people generally remember little of what they either read or hear (as little as 10–20%) but that they retain 50% of what they both see and hear (Shams & Seitz, 2008).

A 2003 study looked at learners' recall of correct answers using touch alone, sight alone, and touch and sight combined (Newell, Bulthoff, & Ernst, 2003). The findings show the advantage of a multisensory approach:

Touch only	65% correct
Sight only	72% correct
Sight and touch	85% correct

The following findings are from a 1960s study that compared the recall of information delivered using unisensory methods with the recall of information delivered using multisensory methods (Dale,

1969). The period between presentation of the material and testing for recall was two weeks. Participants read silently, heard the information from a lecturer, or both heard and saw images that supported the information.

Read only   10% recalled correctly
Heard only   20% recalled correctly
Heard and saw   50% recalled correctly

In a series of studies, Mayer and Anderson (1992) showed that students who took in new information using more than one sensory pathway produced 50% more creative solutions to problems they had been assigned than students using only a unisensory process.

The Power of Smell

Smells are powerful memory makers. Walk into your old high school gym, science lab, or auditorium and see if the smells don't transport you back in time. The part of our brain that handles smell, the piriform cortex, is located directly next to the part responsible for memory and emotion (Herz & Engen, 1996). As a result, our memories are intrinsically and strongly linked with odor. Smell can evoke the emotions surrounding an experience, and it can prompt and even re-create those emotions.

What does this mean for learning? In using smells as cues to enhance recall, you want a smell you like and can positively associate with what you are learning. Lwin, Morrin, and Krishna (2010) found that after a time delay, scent enhanced recall of verbal information and scent-based retrieval cues helped in the recall of pictures. There have not been many studies on smells and learning, and additional research is needed, but it is clear that certain odors can trigger memories.

In a study done at Harvard University and appearing in the *Journal of Science* in 2007, volunteers who were exposed to the scent of roses as they slept after studying were better able to recall the material they had studied, even without being exposed to the rose scent again. The odor intensified the transfer of information to the hippocampus, the part of the brain responsible for helping to form long-term memories (Rasch, Buchel, Gais, & Born, 2007).

The Power of Sight: Pictures and Images

In a 1998 study, students were found to have three times better recall of visual information over oral information, and six times better recall when the information was presented using both oral and visual methods at the same time rather than just oral methods (Najjar, 1998). Humans are incredible at remembering pictures. Hear a piece of information, and three days later you'll remember 10% of it. Add a picture, and you'll remember 65% (Medina, 2008). From an evolutionary perspective, vision was necessary for early human development. It helped in finding food, identifying predators, and finding a mate (Medina, 2008). Hundreds of thousands of years ago, if you didn't see the large tiger hunting you, you probably didn't get to pass on your genes. Biologist James Zull, author of *The Art of Changing the Brain*, writes, "Images are the easiest thing for the brain to learn." Translating what you are trying to learn into graphs, charts, or pictures is an excellent way to improve learning and recall (Zull, 2002).

Concept Maps

Concept maps are graphical tools for organizing and representing knowledge. They were developed in 1972 by Joseph Novak of Cornell University. Novak needed a better way to represent children's conceptual understandings of science for a research study he was conducting. What emerged was a visual structure that he referred to as a concept map. The value of a concept map is that it allows you to organize and associate information in a hierarchal way and then translate the information from a narrative form into a visual form, creating a multisensory learning process.

Figure 4.1 Concept map. Reprinted with permission from Justin Cooper.

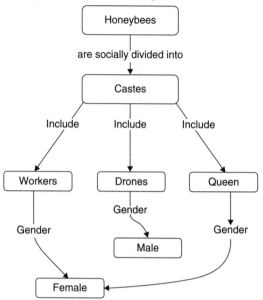

A concept map usually includes circles or boxes containing key words representing the concepts, with connections shown by a line linking two concepts (Figure 4.1). Words on the lines, referred to as linking words or linking phrases, specify the relationship between the two concepts linked by the line. A concept is labeled most often as a word, although sometimes symbols, such as + or %, are used and sometimes more than one word is used (Novak & Canas, 2008).

In concept maps, concepts are represented in a hierarchy with the most inclusive, most general concepts at the top of the map and the more specific, less general concepts arranged hierarchically below (Novak & Canas, 2008). Concept maps also contain cross-links, that is, relationships or links between concepts in different segments or domains of the concept map (see Figure 4.2).

Concept maps are constructed to reflect the organization of a body of information in a visual form. Because vision is the most powerful of our senses, maps are a great way to enhance learning and recall.

Figure 4.2 Cross-links. Reprinted with permission from Justin Cooper.

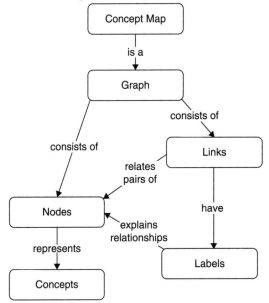

The beauty of a concept map is that it has many possible applications that can enhance learning and memory. The following are several examples of a concept map's use:

- Organizing information to be used in solving a problem
- Making a visual display of a story line
- Classifying the characteristics of a person, place, or thing
- Developing a prewriting outline
- Arranging the contents of a textbook chapter in a visual display (This will allow you to see how the entire chapter is connected before beginning your reading and should lead to improved comprehension.)
- Developing a persuasive argument for a paper
- Presenting the similarities and differences in things
- Showing cause-and-effect processes
- Creating a visual display of class notes

Multisensory Elaboration

Imagine that you had a home separated from a beautiful lake by a large forest. And imagine that you developed a path that you could take each day from your home to the lake. After a time, the path would become worn and easy to follow. Now imagine that a gigantic tree falls across the worn path and blocks your way to the lake. What do you do? You could hire a big guy with a big bulldozer to try to push the tree out of the way—which would be quite expensive—or you could take your chain saw and begin the hard work of cutting up the tree to reopen the path.

This problem could have been prevented altogether had you made several paths from your home to the lake; if one of the paths had become blocked, you could just take another one. The multiple-path scenario is analogous to a method for effectively learning and forming memories for your college work. To create multiple paths to important academic information, you should study and recall course information using multiple senses. Studying in this way creates memory pathways for each of the senses. Thus, you will have many paths to the information, and if one is blocked by test anxiety, fatigue, or just plain forgetfulness, another will likely be available.

The process of creating multiple paths to information is called elaboration. Daniel Schacter (2011), former head of the School of Psychology at Harvard and the author of *The Seven Sins of Memory*, writes, "Whether we like it or not our memories are at the mercy of our elaborations" (p 35). The more ways we can use the information we learn, the more senses we can process it with, the better our chances of recalling it in the future (Schacter, 2001). Using a multisensory approach is one of the best ways to ensure that you can recall information you need when you need it.

Annotation: A Multisensory Approach to Textbook Reading

Ask teachers what drives them crazy about students, and chances are they will answer, "They don't do their readings." Ask students which part of college learning they like the least, and you are likely to get "reading" as the answer. For most individuals, textbooks are hard to read. For most courses, textbooks don't include a story to follow or a mystery to solve. Textbooks for many classes simply list dry facts and definitions. Facts and basic definitions are vital to understanding a subject, but because they are not often fascinating, it can be difficult to maintain your focus on and comprehend the material. Reading textbooks can also be difficult because silent reading is a unisensory experience—only our eyes are involved. In addition, reading is a visually heavy process. In fact, reading is the slowest way humans input information into their brains (Dehaene, 2009). One way to make the reading process easier and more effective is to make it multisensory. You can do this by annotating your text while you read (see Figure 4.3).

Annotation is a simple process of making notes in the margin of the textbook that identify, in your own words, the important concepts, ideas, facts, and details. By using your pencil, you add the sense of touch to the reading process, making it multisensory. And there are two additional benefits of annotation. First, by translating what you are reading into your own words, you are identifying whether you

Figure 4.3 Sample of an annotated textbook page.

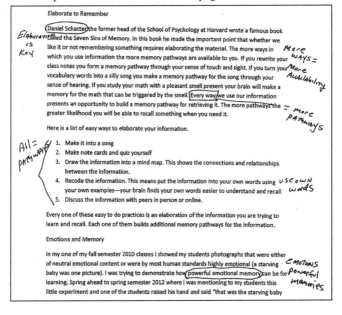

understand what you are reading. If you can't translate the material, you don't yet understand it. The process of translation greatly adds to your comprehension and recall of the text material. Second, using your own words is one of the best ways to make remembering what you read easier. Your own words are your most familiar pattern, and using familiar patterns makes learning easier. (The use of patterns in learning and memory will be explored in the next chapter.)

Learning and recall are made significantly easier when you use a multisensory approach. The more senses involved, the more memory pathways created and the more opportunities to recall the information. If at all possible, never try to learn or study using just one sensory pathway.

Chapter Summary

Following are the key ideas from this chapter:

1. It is likely that the human brain evolved to develop, learn, and operate optimally in multisensory environments. Because multisensory learning gives you more than one way to relate to new information, it's an ideal way to learn.
2. Those in multisensory environments always learn better than those in unisensory environments. They have more recall with better resolution that lasts longer. Learning is evident even 20 years later.
3. Smell is a powerful aid in learning and recall.
4. Vision is the most powerful of all the human senses. The easiest thing for the human brain to recall is an image.
5. Elaboration leads to improved recall. If you use many sensory pathways, you increase the chances of recalling what you learn.

References

Dale, E. (1969). Cone of experience. In R. V. Wiman (Ed.), *Educational media: Theory into practice*. Columbus, OH: Charles Merrill.

Dehaene, S. (2009). *Reading in the brain: The science and evolution of a human invention*. New York: Penguin.

Herz, R. S., & Engen, T. (1996). Odor memory: Review and analysis. *Psychonomic Bulletin and Review, 3*(3), 300–313.

Lwin, M. O., Morrin, W., & Krishna, A. (2010). Exploring the superadditive effects of scent and pictures on verbal recall: An extension of dual coding theory. *Journal of Consumer Psychology, 20,* 317–326.

Mayer, R. E., & Anderson, R. B. (1992). The instructive animation: Helping students build connections between words and pictures in multimedia learning. *Journal of Educational Psychology, 84*(4), 444–452.

Medina, J. (2008). *Brain rules: 12 principles for surviving and thriving at work, home, and school.* Seattle, WA: Pear Press.

Najjar, L. J. (1998). Principles of educational multimedia user interface design. *Human Factors, 40*(2), 311–323.

Newell, F., Bulthoff, H. H., & Ernst, M. (2003). Cross-modal perception of actively explored objects. In Proceedings of EuroHaptics, 291–299.

Novak, J., & Canas, A. (2008). *The theory underlying concept maps and how to construct and use them.* Institute for Human and Machine Cognition. Retrieved from http://cmap.ihmc.us/Publications/ResearchPapers/Theory Cmaps/TheoryUnderlyingConceptMaps.htm

Rasch, B., Buchel, C., Gais, S., & Born, J. (2007, March 9). Odor cues during slow wave sleep prompt declarative memory consolidation. *Science,* 1333. doi:10.1126/science.315.5817.1333k

Schacter, D. L. (2001). *The seven sins of memory: How the mind forgets and remembers.* Boston: Houghton Mifflin.

Shams, L., & Seitz, A. (2008). Benefits of multisensory learning. *Trends in Cognitive Science, 12*(11), 411–417.

Zull, J. (2002). *The art of changing the brain.* Sterling, VA: Stylus.

5

PATTERNS AND LEARNING

Harvard psychiatrist John Ratey, in his book *A User's Guide to the Brain*, describes the human brain "as a pattern seeking device." He writes, "The brain works by relating whole concepts to one another and looks for similarities, differences and relationships between them" (Ratey, 2001, p. 5). One way to enhance learning of new material is using patterns that are already familiar to you.

Let's do a simple demonstration. If you were asked to learn a series of 10 numbers—for example, 2 3 1 7 9 6 4 5 6 0—would you find it easier to memorize this unrelated string, or would you find it easier to memorize them if they were grouped into the following patterns:

(231) 796-4560
2,317,964,560

I have asked more than 2,000 students this question, and essentially all of them have indicated that the 10 numbers are much easier to recall when inserted into a more familiar pattern, such as a phone number or a big number. The pattern itself makes the task easier. You have been using phone numbers and learning big numbers for many years. These familiar patterns give new information greater meaning, which makes it easier to recall.

Here is another example: How difficult would it be for you to learn the following sequence of alternating numbers and letters? They can be recalled in any particular order: 3 A 1 U 5 I 9 E 7 O. Try finding the pattern, and then estimate how difficult it would be to recite these letters and numbers a week from today, with no practice. What if the cue a week later was "odd numbers and vowels"? Again, with no practice, most people could recall all of these numbers and letters (1, 3, 5, 7, 9 and A, E, I, O, U) with no practice. Because this sequence fits a pattern you know well, it is an easy task.

Playing Chess

The value of using patterns can be illustrated when learning to play chess. If someone new to chess learns only the surface of the game—the names of the pieces, how each piece moves, and the rules—he or she can play a game of chess. However, these chess basics don't adequately describe how chess is played; novice players with only this information could not recognize the patterns within the game that would tell them what moves to make or not make. They can "play," but they can't have a real strategy for getting better because all their cognitive effort is tied up thinking about how each piece moves. Adrian de Groot, the Dutch chess master and psychologist, said great chess players are great because of their knowledge of the patterns of possible chess moves. The more patterns they recognize, the better players become (de Groot, 1965).

The human thinking process involves actively creating linkages among concepts, skill elements, people, and experiences in order to make meaning by establishing and reworking patterns, relationships, and connections (Ewell, 1997). We use patterns constantly. (See Box 5.1 for an example of how patterns create meaning and make things easier to learn and remember.) Our brain patterns also change constantly. Every time we learn something new, we first try to alter some previously established patterns (assimilation), and if that does not work, we create additional, new patterns (accommodation) (Atherton, 2011). Patterns are so much a part of how our brains work that when we feel like we don't have command of our own fate, our brains often invent patterns that offer a sense of control (Whitson & Galinsky, 2008). For example, if a friend does something unexpected, it takes only seconds for your mind to start thinking up a reason for the behavior. Your brain is trying to determine a pattern to account for the surprising behavior. As you know, even if we are frequently wrong

---

BOX 5.1
Using Patterns to Make Learning Easier

Note the possible ways to pattern the following words to make them easier to learn and recall:
olives tomatoes bread carrots chicken lettuce cookies ham grapes beef strawberries spinach pork plums mangoes potatoes onions fish duck broccoli cheese cherries brownies turkey

Alphabetical

This is a familiar pattern, but it doesn't help very much:
    Beef, bread, brownies, carrots, cheese, cherries, etc.

A More Meaningful Pattern

Categorizing food words by familiar meals, such as lunch and dinner, gives them more meaning and makes it much easier to recall them. Most everyone would know what is in a salad, a fruit salad, or a dinner entrée. The more connections and the more meaning, the easier it is to learn and recall.

    Lunch: a salad, including lettuce, cheese, tomatoes, olives, carrots, spinach, broccoli, onions, turkey, and ham, with bread and cookies for dessert.

    Dinner: a fruit salad with plums, strawberries, mangoes, grapes, and cherries; choices of duck, chicken, beef, fish, or pork, with potatoes; and a brownie for dessert.

in our assumptions, we can't seem to stop our brains from looking for these types of connections.

Chunking Information

Patterns work so well in learning primarily because they allow you to "chunk" new material—that is, to combine bits of information into a cohesive whole. Psychologists noted a long time ago that your brain can process only a certain amount of material at any given time. Amazingly, this limitation is not based on a specific amount of information or material but rather on a number of chunks of material. One of the most cited works in all psychology is about chunking and the idea that the average human can maintain "seven plus or minus two" chunks of information at any given time (Miller, 1956). Although others have argued that we can hold only a small even number of chunks of information (Gobet & Clarkson, 2004), the importance of getting information into patterns, which form chunks, remains.

Chunking can greatly increase the amount of information you can process. For example, look at the following letters for just a few seconds, cover the letters, and see how many you can remember:

k s b c e w l o h n

Even if you do get all ten letters, note the energy needed to do so.

Now try this again. Same as last time. Look at the following letters for a few seconds, cover them, and see how many you can recall.

f l a s h l i g h t

Of course this example is much easier. The difference between the two sets of letters is that in the second case, there is only one chunk of information. Patterns allow you to find chunks, and chunks allow you to process much more information. This is why if you can find patterns in material you are studying, and thus create chunks, it is much easier to learn and to remember.

Familiar Movie Patterns

Following is a list of the ten most common patterns of modern movies:

1. Horror movie with a psycho killer
2. Buddy cop film
3. Action movie
4. Romance
5. The twist
6. Stereotype shakeup
7. Epic war movie
8. Teen comedy
9. Outrageous comedy
10. The underdog

These established patterns allow you to easily follow movies and make sense of what is happening. If the story follows a pattern too closely, the movie is highly predictable and disappointing. Directors often alter the pattern within the story line to surprise us—which is where plot twists emerge—and make the film more interesting. However, some patterns are universally followed, and if they are violated, moviegoers are very unhappy. If both partners are killed in a buddy cop movie and the "bad" person escapes, people will be displeased with the movie. This story line would violate the standard underlying pattern of the movie.

In the same way that directors use movie-plot patterns, you can use your knowledge of patterns to anticipate what will come next in a class lecture and to help you to follow the new information. This will make it easier for you to understand and recall new information. Without familiar patterns, new information is more difficult to follow and understand, and you will need to take more time and apply more effort to find the meaning.

Most Familiar Patterns

What are some of the most familiar patterns to college students? Gestalt psychologists studied patterns in the 1930s and found that some patterns were essentially universal for all individuals (Koffka,

1935). These patterns still hold true today. Three that are particularly important to learning in school are similarity, figure-ground, and proximity.

Similarity

Look at Figure 5.1. What do you see? Most individuals report seeing columns of the letter X and the letter O. It would be just as easy to "see" rows made up of the letters X and O, but the brain clusters similar items and then makes sense of them by making columns.

In most schools in the United States, teachers capitalize on this inherent sense of similarity and teach students to look for similarities and differences in new material. This can be important to you when you study. If you look for similarities in material, it will be much easier for you to recall the information when it is needed, such as on exam day. Your brain is familiar with the similarity pattern and is used to using it.

Think about learning any new concept. It will often be easier if you first consider how the new concept is similar to other concepts that you already know. It is easier because the part of the new concept that is similar to your old learning is not entirely new; it's familiar. What you are being asked to learn is just the part that is different from the concepts you already know. The learning task is less difficult when you begin it by using this simple pattern.

The next time you are asked to list three similarities and three differences between two plays know that this task is based on Gestalt laws of perceptual organization, a way of finding similarities that is inherent in the brains of just about everyone in the United States.

Figure 5.1 Similarity example.

```
X   O   X   O   X   O

X   O   X   O   X   O

X   O   X   O   X   O

X   O   X   O   X   O

X   O   X   O   X   O
```

Figure-Ground

Another principle that is often used in school is figure-ground. Your brain, like everyone else's brain, is wired to look for the focal point of patterns. When you look at something, you identify a point on which to focus (figure) and the rest of the image or vision becomes the background (ground). If you look at an image, you immediately establish a focal point. In the case of a story, the figure may be the main character and the ground may be the circumstances in which the main character finds himself or herself. For example, what do you see in Figure 5.2?

If the "figure" is the woman, then the large light area is seen as a mirror. However, if the "figure" is a skull, the woman's head becomes the eyes.

When you study, determining what is the "figure" and what is "ground" is extremely important. Keep asking yourself, What in this material is most important?

Proximity

Items in our life are separated by time and space. Our brains see things that are close to one another, either in space or in time, as going together

Figure 5.2 "All Is Vanity," by Charles Gilbert (1892). From www.sandlotsci ence.com/Ambiguous/All_is_Vanity1.htm. ©2013 by SandlotScience.com

Figure 5.3 Proximity example.

XOXOXO

XOXOXO

XOXOXO

XOXOXO

and things that are far apart as distinct. Look at Figure 5.3. Do you see columns of letters, or do you now see rows because of proximity? Note that this is the same "pattern" of six letters in each row for five rows as appeared in Figure 5.1. This time the pattern has different spacing, and so proximity overpowers similarity.

As an example, suppose you are having a party and Joe walks in the door. Then, about 20 min later Sarah walks through the door. Your brain would typically not place Joe and Sarah together. Steve walks in the door about 5 min after Sarah, and Sam 10 s later. In that instant, without any purposeful work on your part, your brain would make the assumption that Steve and Sam came to the party together. Your brain establishes patterns quickly and then starts to construct meaning.

You establish similar patterns when you process course material as well. If your history professor talks about George Washington and then shortly afterward talks about the starting of a new nation, your brain will quickly assume that George Washington had something to do with the new country, even if you were not told this explicitly.

In addition, when events typically happen in close proximity, our brains often infer a cause-and-effect relationship. This assumption makes sense, as causes are often close to their respective outcomes. For example, if you see a person fall down and then seconds later notice a few marbles on the floor, your brain will quickly assume that the marbles caused the person to fall. This is why when something bad happens people believe it is a bad idea to be anywhere in the area. People's brains are prewired to assume that they themselves are associated with the bad event and maybe even that they caused it. This cause-and-effect relationship determined by proximity is important in learning.

Proximity is one reason that it is a good idea not to schedule classes back-to-back and also to take a short break between study sessions when switching from one course curriculum to another. New information can become confusing if learned close to other new information because your brain will often try to establish patterns, even if none exist. This is particularly true when the subjects are relatively close. If you are taking both physics and math in the same semester, it might be helpful to put some space between the class sessions and study sessions for the two courses.

Proximity can also be used to your advantage. If you have complex material to learn, it is important to block off some time during which you can concentrate on that information. If people, a television program, or texts from friends distract you while you are studying, the material will lose its proximity, become less connected, and therefore be harder to learn.

Cause and Effect

What were the causes of the American Civil War, the Vietnam War, or the recent great recession in the United States? What caused the AIDS epidemic or black plague? What are the causes of unrest in the Middle East? What effects can be attributed to phenomena such as global climate change or the counterculture movement of the sixties? What were the effects of the civil rights movement of the fifties and sixties, Hurricane Katrina in New Orleans, or the H1N1 flu scare? Students are asked to explore the causes and effects of events as a regular part of their K–12 learning experiences, both in and outside of school. I recall being asked by Sister Mary what caused the fight on the playground in fourth grade (someone hit "Bigs Main" with a snowball). As expected, she looked for the cause by talking to anyone in close proximity to the incident. I also recall the effects of fighting in fourth grade, when I had to make 100 snowballs with my bare hands and without my coat or hat on.

Cause-and-effect papers are among the most common assignments in any composition course. It is a pattern teachers use because they know students are familiar with it. More simplistic thinking looks for immediate proximity to explain cause-and-effect relationships. A great deal more thinking is involved in finding relationships that are not obvious by simple patterns of close proximity. In college, students are expected to go beyond basic or surface reasons when finding a cause or explaining an effect. For example, if you were assigned a paper on the causes of AIDS, you would be expected to discuss not only that AIDS may be caused in individuals by sexual contact or blood exchanges but also that the disease is caused by a retrovirus that multiplies in the human immune system's CD4+ T cells and kills vast numbers of the cells it infects (Peckham, Jeffries, Quinn, Newell, & Slowik, 2013). Or that the spread of AIDS in children in many parts of Africa is closely related to the health of the mother in the household. Mothers typically protect their daughters from sexual encounters at a young age. When mothers die or are sick, young girls are typically put into sexual situations and AIDS spreads (Peckham et al., 2013). The pattern of cause and effect, particularly when not obvious, is used to promote deeper exploration of ideas and events that require more critical thinking than sorting information into categories.

Other Patterns Commonly Used for Learning

In addition to similarity, figure-ground, proximity, and cause and effect, most students have spent a great deal of time using each of the following organizational structures in their learning:

Hierarchy. In a hierarchy, information is organized in order of importance, from best to worst, biggest to smallest, newest to oldest, and so on. Flow charts, timelines, outlines, and concept maps are common tools used to illustrate hierarchy to aid learning. Thinking of ways to sort information into categories and then to break the information in those categories into subcategories often facilitates learning.

Alphabetical order. From the time you entered preschool, you have been exposed to the pattern of alphabetical order. Just ask anyone whose name begins with an *A* or a *Z*. If you enter "organizing by alphabetical order" into a search engine, you can find websites that will alphabetize material for you at the click of a button. This pattern will not enhance your understanding of the information or show meaningful relationships between pieces of information, but it is so familiar that it may help you to get started when learning new terms or vocabulary words.

Your own language: The most important and familiar pattern for you is your own language. The specific ways in which you use, order, personalize, and abbreviate your language create patterns that are easier for you to recognize and recall. If you take definitions that you need to learn and put them into your own language—a process called recoding—or make up your own example to illustrate a concept, you will find that it is much easier to recall the information. Your brain has been recognizing your own language since you began to speak, and the pattern is very familiar.

Suppose you were asked to explain the definition of the word *epiphany*. Dictionary.com defines *epiphany* as "a sudden, intuitive perception of or insight into the reality or essential meaning of something, usually initiated by some simple, homely, or commonplace occurrence or experience" (http://dictionary.reference.com/browse/epiphany?s=t). It will be much easier to remember this definition if you put it in your own words—for example, "An epiphany is suddenly realizing how something works or what it means and is triggered when you look at or hear something familiar." Not only are your own words easier to remember, but the act of putting the definition in your own words demonstrates that you understand the meaning.

Reading Patterns and Textbooks

Another time to take advantage of patterns in your learning is when you are asked to read textbook material. Textbooks use consistent patterns to display information. For example, almost every textbook has the same format:

Topic
Headings
Subheadings
Paragraphs containing the main idea (which is almost always
    stated in the first sentence), followed by the details, followed
    by examples

This pattern holds true for 90% of the text material you will be asked to read. Knowing this pattern means you know exactly where to look for the important information (the main idea and significant details). It also means you know what parts of the paragraph you might be able to skim or skip over (the examples). Examples are important only if you don't understand the main idea or significant details. Otherwise, they can be skipped, which will speed up your reading and help you to stay focused on the important information—the main ideas, significant details, and important examples (the figure, not the ground).

It is unfortunate that many teachers tell students that everything in the textbook is important and should be read; this is simply not true. Teachers themselves would not read everything. They would focus on the information they want to know and skip everything else. This is how professionals read everything. Read your textbook with these patterns in mind, and you will save time and be a better reader.

Patterns in Other Kinds of Reading

Almost everything you will be assigned to read in school will have a specific pattern to it. Novels have a common pattern that often looks as follows:

The beginning:

1. Introduces the characters
2. Establishes the situation
3. States the conflict
4. Poses the story question or establishes the situation (which should lead to the premise)

The middle—a progression of consequential events, involving the characters, who change as a result of those events:

1. Each event must lead toward resolution of the conflict
2. Each event must reveal more about the characters
3. Each event must relate to the premise

The end:

1. The climax, or the pivotal event that resolves the conflict and proves the premise
2. The resolution, which relates to the premise and answers the story question, if the answer is not obvious as a result of the climax

Knowing the pattern of a novel can keep you focused and enhances your ability to understand the nuances of the plot. The patterns help you to follow the story and anticipate what will come next, and this leads to improved understanding and better concentration and focus.

Although there are several variations on how material is patterned in magazines, the following outline is a common pattern that can help you follow an article and make your reading more productive:

Title
Thesis statement (big idea)
Details from old idea or background information
Transition to new idea
New idea
Background
Transition from background material to supporting evidence
    for new idea
First support
Transition from first support to second support
Second support
Statement of alternatives
Conclusion

With professional journals, as with all written material, there are predictable patterns, but they will vary from subject area to subject area. The best solution to improving your journal-reading skills is to ask either a librarian or your professor for assistance in understanding how the journal is patterned. Also ask your professor how he or she reads a journal. When searching for specific findings, many professionals read research journals in the following order: title, abstract, discussion, methods, results, conclusion, and then introduction. It may vary a bit from person to person, but unless an individual is reading the research journal for fun and general information (yes, people do that), few professionals read journal articles from beginning to end.

Chapter Summary

This chapter discussed how the human brain is a pattern-seeking device that tries to connect concepts and ideas to prior knowledge by looking for the similarities and differences between new information and what the learner already knows. Recognizing the power of patterns in learning helps students to improve their comprehension of what they hear, see, and read and to recall the information more easily and in less time. Following are the key ideas from this chapter:

1. The human brain evolved to deal with patterns.
2. Patterns are everywhere in our daily life.
3. Recognizing patterns in information is essential to improving understanding and recall.
4. Some of the most common patterns are similarity and difference, proximity, figure-ground, cause and effect, and your own language.
5. Knowing the pattern of the subject you are trying to learn will make it easier for you to follow a lecture, to pay attention by anticipating what will come next, and to improve your ability to connect ideas and concepts to things you already know.
6. Textbooks are organized into a pattern of heading, subheading, and paragraphs, which contain main ideas, significant details, and examples. The main idea will be the first sentence of the paragraph the vast majority of the time. Recognizing this defined pattern makes reading easier and faster. If you don't recognize the pattern in what you are being asked to learn or read, ask for help. Knowing the pattern of the material makes learning and recall easier.

References

Atherton, J. S. (2011). *Learning and teaching: Assimilation and accommodation.* Retrieved from http://www.learningandteaching.info/learning/assimacc.htm

de Groot, A. D. (1965). *Thought and choice in chess.* Amsterdam: Noord-Hollandsche Uitgeversmaatschappij.

"Epiphany." *Dictionary.com.* Retrieved from http://dictionary.reference.com/browse/epiphany?s=t

Ewell, P. T. (1997). *Organizing for learning: A point of entry.* Retrieved from http://www.intime.uni.edu/model/learning/learn_summary.html

Gobet, F., & Clarkson, G. (2004). Chunks in memory: Evidence for the magical number four . . . or is it two? *Memory, 12*(6), 732–747.

Koffka, K. (1935). *Principles of Gestalt psychology.* New York: Harcourt Brace.

Miller, G. A. (1956). The magical number seven, plus or minus two: Some limits on our capacity for processing information. *Psychological Review, 63*(2), 81–97.

Peckham, C., Jeffries, D., Quinn, T., Newell, M. L., & Slowik, G. (2013). What is AIDS? *AIDS and Women.* Retrieved from http://ehealthmd.com/library/aidswomen/AID_whatis.html

Ratey, J. (2001). *A user's guide to the brain.* New York: Pantheon Books.

Whitson, J. A., & Galinsky, A. (2008, October 3). Lacking control increases illusory pattern perception. *Science, 322*(5898), 115–117. doi:10.1126/science.1159845

6

MEMORY

When you sing along with the radio, do you ever think about how you learned the lyrics? Did you practice the lyrics at length? Did you make up flash cards and have a friend quiz you? Did your parents or a teacher make up a test over the song lyrics to see if you knew them well? It is unlikely you learned the songs in any of these traditional academic ways. Most likely, without even thinking about it, you just realized one day that you were singing along—even if you often claimed to others that you hated the song.

Usually, when learning something new, it helps to be interested in it, see a value to it, pay a lot of attention to it, and practice it a lot. The human brain is wired to more easily learn things that are "important," and for the most part, what's important is also interesting. So how do we end up learning all these songs we don't want to know? The simple answer is repetition. You heard the song over and over and over. Actually, you didn't just learn the lyrics; you overlearned them. A person will overlearn something when he or she is exposed to that thing many more times after he or she has learned it.

By singing along with the song on the radio, you were doing something else that is important in learning and memory: you were using the

71

learned information. To remember what you need to know in school, you need to have repeated exposure to the material and then you need to use it. This strengthens both the memory and the cues for recovering the memory so that you can use the information when you need it.

Another important aspect of learning is using new material over an extended period. You have probably heard on many occasions (and even in earlier chapters of this book) that it is better to spread out your study sessions rather than cram the night before the test. Cramming for an exam can be described as massed practice. Distributed practice, in contrast, is repeatedly studying and using material over an extended period, such as days, weeks, and even months. Practicing a list of words for 30 min once per day for a week is an example of distributed practice. Studying the list of words for 2 hr straight but only once is an example of massed practice.

If you are like most students, although you know distributed practice is better, you do quite well by cramming. The catch is that material you studied by cramming is much easier to forget because the retrieval cues for that material are not well established. This is something researchers have demonstrated repeatedly. Massed and distributed learning are two different concepts, and you need to know how to do both to be successful in college.

Each time your brain is exposed to, say, the concept of mitosis in your biology class, your memory for mitosis is strengthened. Every time you retrieve a memory—for example, by explaining mitosis to someone—that memory becomes stronger and more readily available. The more times you retrieve the memory (particularly over time), the stronger it is and the more likely you will be able to remember it when you need to. This principle allowed you to learn the lyrics even though you didn't try to learn them and didn't want to know them. You simply heard them and sang along so many times that they became strong memories.

Memory and Sleep

Most researchers now agree that one of the mysteries about how the human brain makes memories has finally been solved. Recently, researchers figured out that memories are made while you sleep. Try a short experiment: Pay attention to how much you remember from the previous day's learning on days when you do not get enough sleep and still feel tired. Compare your recall on tired days to that on days after you've had a full night of restful sleep. If your findings are similar to most recent research findings, you will notice that you remember a great deal more new information when you have had a full night's sleep than when you have been sleep deprived.

What Happens While You Sleep

György Buzsaki, professor at the Center for Molecular and Behavioral Neuroscience at Rutgers University, and his coresearchers have determined that short transient brain events, called sharp wave ripples, are responsible for consolidating memories and transferring new information from the hippocampus, which is a fast-learning but low-capacity short-term memory store, to the neocortex, which is a slower-learning but higher-capacity long-term memory store (Buzsaki, Girardeau, Benchenane, Wiener, & Zugaro, 2009). Information stored in the neocortex will be more stable and have a greater likelihood, if practiced, of becoming long-term memories (see Figure 2.1). Buzsaki et al. (2009) also found that this movement of information happens primarily when we are asleep.

Dr. James Maas, presidential fellow and past chair of psychology at Cornell University, indicates in *Sleep for Success*, the book he wrote with Rebecca Robbins, that sleep has a big impact on memory (Maas & Robbins, 2011). Maas's findings indicate that the final 2 hr of sleep, from hour 5.5 to 7.5 or hour 7 to 9, are crucial for memories to be laid down as stable residents in your brain. During this period in REM sleep, your brain replays scenes from the day over and over again so that they become stable in your memory (Maas & Robbins, 2011).

Preparation for the Next Day's Learning

Sleep also serves other functions. In addition to providing opportunity to consolidate learned material, sleep allows your brain to clear space for new learning to occur the next day. UC Berkeley researchers have found compelling evidence that during sleep 12- to 14-Hz bursts of brain waves, called sleep spindles, may be networking between key regions of the brain to clear a path for learning (Walker, 2005). These electrical impulses help to shift memories from the brain's hippocampus—which has limited storage space—to the nearly limitless prefrontal cortex's "hard drive," thus freeing up the hippocampus to take in fresh data (new learning).

Matthew Walker says that sleep is the key to having a brain that is ready to learn ("Naps Clear the Mind," 2010). Bryce Mander, a postdoctoral fellow in psychology at UC Berkeley and lead author of a study on sleep spindles, adds, "A lot of that spindle-rich sleep is occurring the second half of the night, so if you sleep six hours or less, you are shortchanging yourself and impeding your learning" (as cited in HealthDay News, 2011). Mander goes on to say, "This discovery indicates that we not only need sleep after learning to consolidate what we've memorized, but that we also need it before learning, so that we can recharge and soak up new information the next day" (as cited in HealthDay News, 2011).

Remembering What We Think Is Important

Your brain will make memories of the information it recognizes as important. Sometimes your brain has to determine what is important. Think about what is likely to be important in your life. Things that we do and say over and over must be important or we wouldn't waste energy or time repeating them. Information needed for survival—for example, asking your loved one, "Did you take your medication today?"—is important, as is information about friends and family. Material processed when you are excited also tends to be judged important by the brain.

You will also recall well what you learn or process just before going to sleep, for two reasons. First, the material is fresh in your mind. Second, other information did not displace or interfere with the material before you drifted off to sleep. In a 2012 study, Dr. Jessica Payne and her colleagues found that people who studied material right before they went to sleep each night made stronger memories for that information (Payne et al., 2012). Provided that you are not totally exhausted, 20 min of review right before bed is great for strengthening recall.

Taking Classes Back-to-Back and Memory

Sleep is important for consolidation, but it is not the only time the brain is strengthening connections to information. Researchers Tambini, Ketz, and Davachi of New York University's Department of Psychology and Center for Neural Science discovered that the parts of the brain that are active during new learning continue to be active up to an hour following the end of that learning. This finding demonstrates the importance of postexperience rest (resting after new learning) in creating memories for recent experiences (Tambini, Ketz, & Davachi, 2010). The brain needs additional time to process the new learning, make important connections, and strengthen the cues to the information just learned. Thus, it is helpful to relax after learning, rather than learn additional information right away. Research has shown that recall of new information was improved in people who were given a break after learning (Tambini et al., 2010).

Cramming, Learning, and Distributed Practice

Dozens of studies show it is possible to cram for an exam and do well on that exam (Wheeler, Ewers, & Buonanno, 2003). Studying intensely for an extended period can help the brain to remember a lot of information for a short period. The key part of this statement is "a short period"— typically 18–36 hr. Unfortunately, cramming requires a great deal of effort but provides no long-term learning benefits. Research about cramming shows that as little as a day or two following a cram session, you will no longer remember a great deal of the information you studied. Within a week, you will likely have forgotten 75% or more of the material you studied (Krishnan, 2013). You quickly forget the information because your brain did not make any long-term memories for it. For information to become a part of your long-term memory, it has to be practiced many times over an extended period. This is called distributed practice. Cramming fails to produce long-term learning because the time frame for studying is too short to build the kind of memory that will last.

The practice of cramming also signals to the brain that the information being studied is not important. After you take an exam you've crammed for, you usually have an exhausted, "I am glad that is over" feeling. This feeling tells the brain that the information is no longer needed and can be purged as you sleep. Of course, cramming typically leads to fatigue, and we have already discussed the difficulty of learning when tired. Taken altogether, many factors make cramming a short-term solution without any real positive long-term outcomes. As one group of researchers put it, "If learning is your goal cramming is an irrational act" (Jang, Wixted, Pecher, Zeelenberg, & Huber, 2012, p. 973).

Following is a quick story from my own life to illustrate this point: When I was an undergraduate, I took two years of Spanish and earned an A in all courses. I also lived in a Spanish-speaking country for a year following college. Yet today I know only about 30 words of Spanish. Why? Because I crammed for all my Spanish exams, and when I lived abroad, I tried my best to find people who spoke English to hang out with. I never engaged in distributed practice with my Spanish, and for all my time, money, and cramming, I got 30 words. If your goal is to actually learn something, cramming does not work.

Practice Makes Knowledge and Skills Available When We Need Them

A good example of distributed practice is daily review or recall of course information. As happened with the song lyrics, if you retrieve from your memory the material you are trying to learn each day, even if it's for only a short period, your brain will make a pathway to that information that is easier and easier to access.

Learning and memory have two key components: the learned object itself and the retrieval cue to find the learned material. Think of it this way: There are many books in the library, and to find a specific book about a specific topic, you first look up the call number and then go to where the book is shelved. If the book has been misshelved, the library doesn't have it, or you don't know how to look up the topic, then you can't get to the book. Finding a book in a library is similar to accessing a retrieval cue. Researchers have found that both the memory itself (the book) and the retrieval cue (the call number) are needed for you to remember something.

The best way for you to strengthen both the memory and the cue is to review material on a regular basis over an extended period—a few weeks at least. To make good use of your study time, don't just look over the material or read over the material passively, but actually try to recall the material. Each time a memory is recalled, both it and its cue are strengthened, and you can access the desired information in your brain faster. Simply reading the material over is much less effective in building a strong memory process.

Elaboration

Daniel Schacter, former head of the School of Psychology at Harvard, wrote a book titled *The Seven Sins of Memory*, in which he stressed that whether we like it or not, remembering something requires elaboration of the material (Schacter, 2001). Decorations can be made more elaborate, stories can be made more elaborate, jewelry can be made more elaborate, and information can be made more elaborate. In each of these cases, elaboration has the same effect: more impact. The more ways in which you elaborate on, or connect, information, the more memory pathways are available to you. If you rewrite your class notes, you form a memory pathway through your sense of touch and sight. If you turn your vocabulary words into a silly song, you make a memory pathway for the song through your sense of hearing. If you study your math with a scented candle burning, your brain will make a memory for the math that can be triggered by the candle's smell. If you study both the text-book definition of a word and a definition written in your own words, your brain will store both meanings. Each way we use our information presents an opportunity to build a memory pathway for retrieving it.

The more pathways, the greater the likelihood you will be able to recall something when you need it.

The following is a list of easy ways to elaborate your information:

1. Make it into a song.
2. Make flash cards and quiz yourself.
3. Draw the information into a concept map. This shows the connections and relationships between the information.
4. Recode the information—that is, put the information into your own words using your own examples. Your brain finds your own words easier to understand and recall.
5. Discuss the information with peers in person or online.

Every one of these simple practices is a way to elaborate the information you are trying to learn and recall. Each one of them builds additional memory pathways for the information.

Emotions and Memory

In a fall semester class, I showed my students photographs with either neutral emotional content (e.g., cars driving down the road) or highly emotional content (e.g., a starving baby). Through this exercise, I was trying to demonstrate the power of emotional memory on learning. Two years later I mentioned this experiment to my students in an upper-division class, and one of the students raised his hand and said, "That was the starving baby picture." He had seen the picture only once, but two years later he still recalled it with accuracy. This shows that the brain does better remembering emotional content than neutral content (Perrin et al., 2012).

A study by Bloom, Beal, and Kupfer (2003) showed that emotional arousal organizes and coordinates brain activity. When the amygdala (a structure located deep within the brain, primarily responsible for processing memory of emotional reactions) detects emotions, it boosts activity in the areas of the brain that form memories (Gazzaniga, Ivry, & Mangun, 2009). This makes a lot of sense, as all humans have learned that highly emotional events and material are usually important. As learners, anytime you can connect on an emotional level to your new learning by personalizing it or connecting it to an emotional memory, you make it easier to form a memory for the new learning.

Multitasking

Most students today are good at jumping from one task to another. Texting someone while listening to music while doing your math homework—no problem! You might even have the TV on at the same time. It is true that most college students today do a nice job of switching between tasks more rapidly than members of the older generation do. However, there is a big difference between switching from one task to another, or task shifting, and *doing* both tasks at the same time, or multitasking. When you shift tasks while working on something that requires thinking, such as texting your friend and listening to a lecture in class, your brain goes through a four-step process that allows you to switch your attention: (a) shift alert, (b) rule activation for task 1, (c) disengagement, (d) rule activation for task 2 (Medina, 2008, p. 86). This process is repeated every time you switch tasks that involve thinking, and you never get better or faster at it. You may have noticed that when you try to do two thinking tasks at the same time, you cannot complete both simultaneously, as the brain must shut down one task before working on the other. Studies show clearly that when you try to do two thinking activities at once (multitasking), or even to shift quickly between tasks, the results are lousy. Typically, research demonstrates that individuals who shift tasks make 50% more errors and spend at least 50% more time on both tasks (Medina, 2008). That means it takes longer to do a worse job.

Multitasking violates everything scientists know about memory formation (Foerde, Knowlton, & Poldrack, 2006). Your brain is at its best when it is focused on one learning task at a time. Full attention is needed for learning. One study shows that our brains actually try to trick us into thinking we can multitask—but we can't (Dux, Ivanoff, Asplund, & Marois, 2006). Focus on one task at a time, and you'll do better at each task in much less time.

Why Students Forget

Everyone forgets things, especially when people are bombarding their brains with stimulation all day long: texting, phoning, e-mailing, Facebooking, listening to music, playing video games, watching TV, and even studying new information for class. The human brain did not evolve to deal with constant stimulation. Neuroscientist Marc Berman and his colleagues have shown that constant stimulation (walking the busy city streets; headphones on all the time with music playing; continually texting, phoning, gaming, etc.) exhausts the brain and causes it to perform poorly on learning and memory tasks. When our brains are exhausted, it is difficult to remember just about anything (Berman, Jonides, & Kaplan, 2008). Berman's research also showed that exhausted brains make for cranky people. The cure is a 20- to 30-min nap, a quiet walk in the woods (but not the city, which is too full of stimulation), or meditation.

In *The Seven Sins of Memory*, Schacter (2001) notes three main causes of students' forgetfulness:

1. Blocking—Information is stored but can't be accessed at a later time because something is preventing the retrieval of information. This usually results from anxiety, which interferes with pathways in the brain and results in a temporary failure to recall information. Many students have experienced this as test anxiety.
2. Misattribution—A memory is attributed to the wrong situation or source. This memory error may happen when you are taking two or more courses with similar information during the same semester. Taking biochemistry, biology, and physics at the same time, for example, might cause your brain to confuse which class was the source for which information. Try studying for each test in a different room or with a different scent present, and then, during the exam, think of the room you studied for that class in or bring the scent with you to the exam.
3. Transience—Memory is lost over time. In the first hour following a lecture, 65% of the material presented can be lost. Of course, things we learned and have not used for a long time can

be hard to recall, but Schacter is referring to the forgetfulness that comes from not spending enough time studying to form a solid memory of certain material. It takes much more time and effort to create a lasting memory than most people realize. When you do not practice the information enough over an extended period (distributed practice), your brain has no reason to make long-term memories for the information. There is no substitute for practice.

Caffeine, Sugar, and Memory

In two separate studies, participants who used 75 mg of caffeine and 75 mg of sugar together in drink form were found to show improvement in attention and declarative memory tasks without significant changes in mood (Kennedy & Scholey, 2004). Yes, sugar and caffeine can have beneficial impacts on learning and memory. Of course, it is important to note that these benefits are also obtained through aerobic exercise, without all the calories (see chapter 3).

Stress and Memory

For decades scientists have known that long-term stress adversely affects the ability to learn and remember. Only recently was it discovered that even minor stressful events, lasting only a short time, interfere with your ability to learn and remember. Acute stress activates selective corticotropin-releasing hormones (CRHs), which disrupt the process by which the brain collects and stores memories (Baram, Chen, Dubé, & Burgdorff, 2008). The best way to protect yourself from the hazards of stress is to begin exercising. A 2012 study showed that aerobic exercise actually helps the brain repair the damage done from stress and protects the brain from the harmful effects of stress (Ebdrup, 2012). Studying regularly over time and knowing the material is also a great defense against stress in the college classroom. Early studying can, in fact, have a double effect: you will know the material better, and it will be easier to both learn and remember previously learned material because your stress level is down.

Chapter Summary

Following are the key ideas from this chapter:

1. Memories are made during sleep, so sleeping 7.5–9 hr per night is crucial to academic success.
2. Naps can help in memory formation. A 30-min nap helps to stabilize new memories, making them easier to be recalled later.
3. Don't take classes back-to-back. Postexperience rest is important in creating memories for recent experiences.
4. Retrieve a memory to strengthen it. Each time you recall a memory, rather than just studying it, your brain makes it stronger and more easily recalled in the future.
5. Cramming will not help long-term recall.
6. We remember emotionally charged information better than neutral information.
7. Elaborate information to improve recall. The more ways you practice new information, the more memory pathways are made for recalling it.
8. Don't shift tasks when doing tasks that require thinking or energy. When it comes to learning, your brain is at its best when it is doing one thing at a time.
9. Forgetting is likely a result of anxiety, misattribution, or not practicing the information enough to make it into a more permanent memory.

References

Baram, T., Chen, Y., Dubé, C., & Burgdorff, C. (2008, March 13). Short-term stress can affect learning and memory. *ScienceDaily*. Retrieved from http://www.sciencedaily.com/releases/2008/03/080311182434.htm

Berman, M., Jonides, J., & Kaplan, S. (2008, December). The cognitive benefits of interacting with nature. *Psychological Science, 19*, 1207–1212.

Bloom, F., Beal, M., & Kupfer, D. (Ed.). (2003). *The Dana guide to brain health*. New York: Free Press.

Buzsaki, G., Girardeau, G., Benchenane, K., Wiener, S., & Zugaro, M. (2009). Selective suppression of hippocampal ripples impairs spatial memory. *Nature Neuroscience, 12*, 1222–1223. doi:10.1038/nn.2384

Dux, P. E., Ivanoff, J., Asplund, C. L. O., & Marois, R. (2006). Isolation of a central bottleneck of information processing with time-resolved fMRI. *Neuron, 52*(6), 1109–1120.

Ebdrup, N. (2012, January 13). Stress and exercise repair the brain after a stroke. *ScienceNordic*. Retrieved from http://sciencenordic.com/stress-and-exercise-repair-brain-after-stroke

Foerde, K., Knowlton, B., & Poldrack, R. (2006). Modulation of competing memory systems by distraction. *Proceedings of the National Academy of Science, 103*, 11778–11783.

Gazzaniga, M. S., Ivry, R. B., & Mangun, G. R. (2009). *Cognitive neuroscience: The biology of the mind*. New York: W.W. Norton.

HealthDay News. (2011, March 8). *Brain's learning ability seems to recharge during light slumber*. Retrieved from http://www.alegentcreighton.com/body.cfm?id=4794&action=detail&ref=50872

Jang, Y., Wixted, T., Pecher, D., Zeelenberg, R., & Huber, D. (2012). Decomposing the interaction between retention interval and study/test practice. *Quarterly Journal of Experimental Psychology, 65*(5), 962–997.

Kennedy, D. O., & Scholey, A. B. (2004). A glucose-caffeine energy drink ameliorates subjective and performance deficits during prolonged cognitive demand. *Appetite, 42*, 331–333.

Krishnan, K. (2013, May 3). Exam cramming is not learning. *Today*. Retrieved from http://www.todayonline.com/commentary/exam-cramming-not-learning

Maas, J., & Robbins, R. (2011). *Sleep for success*. Bloomington, IN: Authorhouse.

Medina, J. (2008). *Brain rules*. Seattle, WA: Pear Press.

Naps clear the mind, help you learn. (2010, February 21). *Live Science*. Retrieved from http://www.livescience.com/9819-naps-clear-mind-learn.html.

Payne, J. D., Tucker, M. A., Ellenbogen, J. M., Wamsley, E. J., Walker, M. P., Schacter, D. L., & Stickgold, R. (2012). Memory for semantically related and unrelated declarative information: The benefit of sleep, the cost of wake. *PLoS ONE, 7*(3), e33079. doi:10.1371/journal.pone.0033079

Perrin, M., Henaff, M., Padovan, C., Faillenot, I., Merville, A., & Krolak-Salmon, P. (2012). Influence of emotional content and context on memory in mild Alzheimer's disease. *Journal of Alzheimer's Disease, 29*(4), 817–826. doi:10.3233/JAD-2012-111490

Schacter, D. L. (2001). *The seven sins of memory: How the mind forgets and remembers.* Boston: Houghton Mifflin.

Tambini, A., Ketz, N., & Davachi, L. (2010). Enhanced brain correlations during rest are related to memory for recent experiences. *Neuron, 65*(2), 280–290.

Walker, M. (2005). A refined model of sleep and the time course of memory formation. *Behavioral and Brain Science, 28*, 51–104.

Wheeler, M. A., Ewers, M., & Buonanno, J. F. (2003). Different rates of forgetting following study versus test trials. *Memory, 11*, 571–580.

7

MINDSETS TOWARD LEARNING

In addition to adopting the strategies and techniques that will help you grasp and remember information, you need to understand something about yourself as a learner that we believe will result in a fundamental change in the way you learn. Gaining this understanding is so important that it will likely influence many other aspects of your life as well. The information in this chapter relates to a concept researchers call mindset. A mindset is a view you have of yourself as a learner, and it affects all the decisions you make about your learning—the effort you put forth, the risks you take, how you deal with failures and criticism, and how much of a challenge you are willing to accept. Mindset was first described by Dr. Carol Dweck, a psychologist at Stanford University. Dweck (2006, 2009) explains that your view of yourself as a learner was likely formed in middle school (or even earlier) and has been affecting your learning ever since. As you read this chapter, reflect on the concepts presented and try to figure out what kind of mindset you have and how you can develop a mindset that leads to optimal learning for you.

*Fixed mindset & Growth mindset

Mindset and Intelligence

One thing about human intelligence is absolutely certain: it is malleable, meaning it can be changed through exposure to new information or even by looking at what you already know in a new way. There is no limit to what you can learn, and contrary to what some may think, nobody's brain has ever been "filled." The brain continually changes by making new neuroconnections between its cells, which represent new knowledge or skills, and when this happens, we say someone has become smarter. It is possible for humans to become smarter all the time and in any area of study. Some subjects will be harder for you to learn than others, but learning in any area is possible. Intelligence is not a fixed quantity that you got at birth and are stuck with. You become smarter every day, and the intelligence you achieve in your lifetime is unknowable. That said, it does appear that your mindset about learning will have a heavy impact on how much you will learn—and just about everything else in your life.

Your mindset is your view about your own intelligence and abilities. This view affects your willingness to engage in learning tasks and how much, if any, effort you are willing to expend to meet a learning challenge. Dweck has spent more than 30 years researching learners' mindsets and their individual views of their intelligence. She noted that mindsets fall into two categories: "fixed mindsets" and "growth mindsets." A person with a fixed mindset "believes that intelligence is a fixed trait," despite hundreds of studies that have found otherwise. In this view, either you are smart in a given area or you are not; there is nothing you can do to improve in that area. Individuals with fixed mindsets believe their intelligence is reflected in their academic performance (Dweck, 2006). If a student doesn't do well in a class, it's because he or she is not "smart" in that area. Individuals with fixed mindsets mistakenly believe either that they shouldn't need to work hard to do well because the smart students don't have to (although when researchers asked students who consistently achieved high grades about their work, they reported working very hard at academic material) or that putting in the effort won't make any difference in the outcome ("I'm just not good at math"). In fact, individuals with fixed mindsets see putting in effort as indicating that they are not smart. They have falsely come to the conclusion that learning comes easy to the students at the top of the class and that they were born that way.

People with growth mindsets, in contrast, believe that intelligence grows as you add new knowledge and skills. Those with growth mindsets value hard work, learning, and challenges and see failure as a message that they need to change tacks in order to succeed next time. Thomas Edison is reported to have tried hundreds of times before he got the lightbulb to work. At one point, he was asked by a *New York Times* reporter about all his failures and whether he was going to give up. Edison responded, "I have not failed 700 times. I've succeeded in proving 700 ways how not to build a light bulb" (as cited in Ferlazzo, 2011). Shortly after this interview, he was successful, and we have all since benefited from his growth mindset. Individuals with growth mindsets are willing to take learning risks and understand that through practice and effort—sometimes a lot of effort—their abilities can improve. Those with growth mindsets believe that their brains are malleable, that intelligence and abilities constantly grow, and that only time will tell how smart they will become.

Chess Champions

In 2008 three British researchers set out to discover what people who became extraordinary in their fields had in common. Among the people they looked at were the top-10 chess players in the world. One of the criteria they used in their investigation was intelligence, or IQ. The researchers had each of the 10 expert chess players take an intelligence test. They were surprised to discover that 3 of the 10 had below-average IQs. They pondered the obvious question: How could a person be so good at a complex game, which most associate with high intelligence, yet have a low IQ? The answer they found explained how a person becomes an expert: practice. Each of the three players with below-average IQs had played between 10,000 hr and 50,000 hr of chess. Their effort and practice had allowed them to become much better chess players than thousands of other chess players who had higher levels of intelligence. The discovery of the benefits of practice among chess players led researchers to identify many additional cases in which greatness was achieved through thousands of hours and years of practice (Colvin, 2006).

Those studying learning and memory now agree that it is not typically intelligence that makes a person an expert in a given area, but rather effort and practice. Think of a case in which an individual stepped into the spotlight and won a competition, whether it was basketball, race-car driving, chess, or a quiz bowl. It doesn't just happen. In fact, in most news interviews, top athletes commonly talk about how hard they have been working on their game. George Gervin, one of the greatest scorers in National Basketball Association (NBA) history, was known for shooting a thousand jump shots each day. Whether you want to be skilled at an activity or a top scholar in your discipline, having a growth mindset and taking the time to practice are necessary.

The Beginning: Middle School

An individual's mindset begins to surface in middle school, when more stringent academic work appears in the curriculum. Students who in elementary school could be successful with little effort and who were frequently told they were "naturally smart" begin to doubt their abilities when learning challenges increase. Dweck discovered that these students had abilities that inspired learner self-confidence, but only when the going was easy. When setbacks occurred, everything changed. Dweck, with her colleague Dr. Elaine Elliott, discovered that learning goals explained the difference between students who were not stopped by the setbacks and those who saw setbacks as failures to be avoided. According to Dweck (2007a), "the mastery-oriented students [those with growth mindsets] are really hell-bent on learning something" and have strong "learning goals." Learning goals are different from performance goals in an important way. Performance goals are oriented on a specific task, whereas learning goals consider the bigger picture of what is being learned by success or failure. Students for whom performance is paramount are often deterred by failures and attempt to look smart even if it means not learning in the process. These individuals have a fixed mindset and will even put others down when failures happen in order to preserve their self-esteem. For them, each task is a challenge to their self-image, and each setback becomes a personal threat. Often, they pursue only activities at which they're sure to shine—and they avoid the sorts of experiences necessary to grow and flourish in any endeavor (Dweck, 2006, p. 58).

Dweck (2006, p. 47) is careful to point out that learning mindsets are context specific. That is, a person can have a growth mindset in one area and a fixed mindset in another area. You might believe that you cannot do math because you weren't born with "math smarts" and that working harder or getting extra help won't help you to learn math. You might also take guitar lessons and practice your guitar 3 hr a day because you know practice is needed to be good at playing a guitar. In this case, you would hold a fixed mindset for math and a growth mindset for guitar playing. There is no doubt that people have preferences; you may well like playing the guitar and not like math. That said, with respect to intelligence and abilities, practicing math for 3 hr every night for a few months would greatly change your math intelligence.

Another surprising finding from Dweck's 2006 research is that there is no relationship between students' abilities or intelligence and the development of a growth mindset (p. 46). Sometimes students with all As have fixed mindsets. One bright student might develop a fixed mindset while another develops a growth mindset based on the feedback each has received about his or her past performances and current levels of ability. A student with a fixed mindset may have had early successes at math and may have received feedback such as "You are really smart!" or "You are a natural at math. You should be a mathematics teacher!" These types of comments might have given that student the impression that certain subjects come easily to smart people. If you have to work at learning, then you are not smart. This feedback might give a person a fixed mindset for math. The problem will come later, when the math becomes more difficult and hard work is needed to be successful. Now the student might think, "I must not be good at this type of math. Oh, well, effort didn't come into play before when I did well, so effort must not be related to success. I guess I will do something else."

This example student's mindset might have been different if his or her early success was met with comments such as "Look at how well you did. Your hard work really paid off." This feedback should foster a growth mindset and encourage practice in the future. If you are a nontraditional student who has children, you might follow Dweck's advice for parents. She says it is vital for parents to give feedback on their children's successful efforts and learning strategies, not on their intelligence (Dweck, 2006).

The significance of Dweck's research for college students is profound. Each fall, tens of thousands of students enroll in classes that they believe they do not have the ability to pass. They also believe that hiring a tutor, visiting the professor during office hours for extra help, or even working harder will make no difference. They hold this belief because they have a fixed mindset in that area.

The next time you take a class on a subject you fear because you think you are not "smart" in that area, keep in mind that practice can make a huge difference in your learning success. The class may not be easy for you, but if you have some background knowledge in the subject or take time to learn some background information (e.g., through learning development courses or tutoring) and you work hard (keep a growth mindset), there is no telling what you will achieve.

Fixed Mindsets and Laziness

College and university professors often see lack of effort as laziness. Not going to tutoring or taking advantage of a professor's office hours is seen as irresponsible or immature. In fact, it may be that a student's fixed mindset is causing many of his or her problems. If you have always struggled with reading, you may believe it is because you are simply "bad at reading" or "not smart in that way." A person with this mindset sees tutoring and extra work as wasted effort. Other students with similar mindsets may work hard but tell themselves, "This is hard. . . . I can't get it. . . . Maybe I should drop the class." We don't have to tell you that studying with that attitude is not productive at all. In contrast, those with growth mindsets work hard, even on work for classes they don't like, and because they know the effort will likely produce improved results, they see greater success. Those students are not smarter; they just see themselves differently.

Characteristics of Fixed and Growth Mindsets

The following is a list of behaviors for each type of mindset. These lists have been included to help you discover how you view yourself as a learner in the many different areas of your learning life. These lists were compiled based on information from Dr. Michael Richards (2007).

Fixed Mindset

1. **Self-image.** Just about everyone strives to have a positive self-image, even those with fixed mindsets. How do individuals with fixed mindsets, who fail to see value in working to improve, protect their self-image? They take on only easy tasks, try to make others look dumb, and discount others' achievements.

2. **Challenges.** Students with fixed mindsets often stick to what they know they can do well. They avoid other challenges because the potential for failure presents a risk to their self-image. If you are a student who asks, "Are there some easy classes I could take?" you may have a fixed mindset.

3. **Obstacles.** People with fixed mindsets usually use obstacles—or external, uncontrollable roadblocks that make learning harder and are difficult to avoid—as an excuse or avoid them by being absent.

4. **Effort.** People with fixed mindsets view effort as unpleasant and unrewarding; therefore, it is to be avoided. Their perception of "great effort" can fall quite short of what is actually required to achieve academic success. This may also contribute to their view of effort as futile.

5. **Criticism.** For people with fixed mindsets, any criticism of their abilities is seen as criticism of themselves as individuals. Useful criticism is usually ignored or, even worse, seen as an insult. This personal response to criticism leads to less and less chance of improvement because they are not open to using any of the feedback that could help them improve.

6. **Success of others.** Students with fixed mindsets see others' success as making them look bad. They may try to convince their peers that others' success was attributable to luck, an expensive private tutor, or even cheating. They may even try to distract their peers from the success of others by bringing up their own unrelated personal successes or the previous failures of those who are currently successful.

Growth Mindset

1. **Self-image.** Individuals with growth mindsets do not see their self-image as tied to their abilities because they know their abilities can be further developed and improved. They want to learn and accept that failure is an important part of learning, even if they are not creating the lightbulb.

2. **Challenges.** Those with growth mindsets embrace challenges because they believe they will come out stronger for being tested. They believe they will discover valuable things by engaging in the effort of a challenge.

3. **Obstacles.** Because the self-image of a person with a growth mindset is not tied to his or her success or appearance to others, failure is an opportunity to learn. So, in a sense, these people win either way. An obstacle is just one more of many things on the road toward learning and improving.

4. **Effort.** People with growth mindsets see effort as necessary if growth and eventual mastery is to be achieved. It is viewed as a natural part of the learning process.

5. **Criticism.** Students with growth mindsets are not any more thrilled to receive negative criticism than anyone else, but they

know it is not personal and is meant to help them grow and improve. They also see the criticism as directed only at their current level of abilities, which they know will change with time and effort.

6. **Success of others**. The success of others is seen as an inspiration, and their information findings are seen as something to learn from.

Changing to a Growth Mindset

Nearly everyone has at least one fixed mindset, and there are things you can do to change your fixed mindsets into growth mindsets. As was mentioned at the beginning of this chapter, intelligence is malleable and can be changed, meaning you can in fact "grow your brain." Jesper Mogensen, a psychologist at the University of Copenhagen, has found that the brain is like a muscle that gets stronger with use and that learning prompts neurons in the brain to grow new connections (Mogensen, 2012). You need to understand that you are an agent of your own brain development.

Dweck's research has found that students of all ages, from early grade school through college, can learn to have growth mindsets. It is important to recognize that your intellectual skills can be cultivated through hard work, reading, education, the confrontation of challenges, and other activities (Dweck, 2007a). Dweck explains that students may know how to study, but they won't want to if they believe their efforts are futile. If you accept that effort will pay dividends, then you are on your way to greater academic and life success. This does not mean that you will enjoy all subjects that you study, only that everyone can improve as they work in different academic areas. Even your teacher was a novice at one time and had to spend a good deal of time studying in order to become an expert in his or her field. Researcher Joshua Aronson of New York University demonstrated that college students' GPAs go up when they accept that intelligence can be developed (Dweck, 2007b).

The following are several aspects of a growth mindset that are important for you to know:

1. Success most often comes from effort and learning strategies, not intelligence. If intelligence earned you a grade of A on the first test and then you failed the second test, did you suddenly become stupid? Of course not. For the first test, you used the right study strategies and put in enough effort to earn an A. When you failed, something was wrong with your level of effort and strategy. It may be that the material was more difficult and needed additional effort.

2. You can grow your own brain. Neuroscience research findings clearly show that new neuron networks are created and become permanent through effort and practice (Goldberg, 2009; Ratey, 2001). These new networks make us smarter. This knowledge is the key to shifting yourself away from a fixed mindset toward a growth mindset.

3. Failure can point you toward future success. When you fail, focus on the strategies you used and the time and effort you put forth to see what caused the failure. Ask for feedback from the teacher. Taking advantage of failure is a key ingredient in creating a growth mindset. When you focus on how you can improve—by finding a new strategy, getting a study partner, reviewing on a daily basis, or putting in more time and effort— you can discover how to overcome the failure. Your ability to face a challenge is not dependent on your actual skills or abilities; it's based on the mindset you bring to the challenge. You need to be willing to take learning risks and be open to learning all you can from your experiences. This message can be difficult to accept, but it is crucial to your growth and development as a learner.

4. Your performance reflects only your current skills and efforts, not your intelligence, worth, or potential. Weight-lifting improvement comes solely from improved technique and increased effort. The more you practice and the better your technique becomes, the greater the amount of weight you can lift. Being a weakling is simply a current state of performance, not who you are. College classes are often like weight lifting.

You start small, and with repeated practice, you keep building brain muscle.

How to Help Yourself

The way to help yourself is to use self-talk. Carol Dweck (2009) offers the following suggestions:

Step 1. You need to learn to hear your fixed mindset "voice."

Students can learn to listen and recognize when they are engaging in a fixed mindset. Students may say to themselves or hear in their heads things like, "Are you sure you can do it? Maybe you don't have the talent," or, "What if you fail—you'll be a failure." Also, catch yourself exaggerating the situation, as that can signal a fixed mindset. Some individuals indicate they can't do math. Although it is possible geometry, algebra, or calculus might be challenging, it is difficult to believe a college student can't do *any* math. A person with a fixed mindset will say things like, "I can't give presentations."

Step 2. You need to recognize you have a choice.

How you interpret challenges, setbacks, and criticism is a choice. You need to know you can choose to ramp up your strategies and effort, stretch yourself, and expand your abilities. It's up to you.

Step 3. You need to talk back to yourself with a growth mindset voice.

THE FIXED MINDSET says, "Are you sure you can do it? Maybe you don't have the talent."

THE GROWTH MINDSET answers, "I'm not sure I can do it now, but I think I can learn to with time and effort."

FIXED MINDSET: "What if you fail—you'll be a failure."

GROWTH MINDSET: "Most successful people had failures along the way."

Step 4. Students need to take growth mindset action.

The more you choose the growth mindset voice, the easier it will become to choose it again and again.

Chapter Summary

This chapter introduced the concept of mindset to students. It explained what a mindset is and how and when mindset is formed. The chapter also explained how students can determine which kind of mindset they have, fixed or growth, and how they can change to a growth mindset if they need to. Following are the key ideas from this chapter:

1. A mindset is a view you have of yourself as a learner, and it affects all the decisions you make about your learning—the effort you put forth, the risks you take, how you deal with failures and criticism, and how much of a challenge you are willing to accept.

2. Mindset was first described by Dr. Carol Dweck, a psychologist at Stanford University. Dweck explains that this view of yourself as a learner was likely formed in middle school (or even earlier) and has been affecting your learning ever since.

3. One thing about human intelligence is absolutely certain: it is malleable, meaning it can be changed through exposure to new information or even by looking at what you already know in a new way. There is no limit to what you can learn, contrary to what some may think.

4. Dweck noted that individuals' views of themselves as learners fall into two categories: fixed mindsets and growth mindsets.

5. Those with fixed mindsets "believe that intelligence is a fixed trait" (Dweck, 2006, p. 96). In their view, you are either smart in a given area or you are not, and nothing can be done to improve in that area. Students with fixed mindsets usually put forth much less effort in a course if the course is viewed as difficult because they believe they are not smart enough to pass.

6. People with growth mindsets believe that intelligence grows as you add new knowledge and skills. They value hard work, learning, and challenges and see failure as a message that they need to change tacks in order to succeed next time.

7. These views of intelligence begin to surface in middle school, when more stringent academic work appears in the curriculum.

8. Dweck is careful to point out that these mindsets are context specific. That is, a person can have a growth mindset in one area and a fixed mindset in another area.

9. A fixed mindset, which often causes students to put in less effort and to avoid going to tutoring or using a professor's office hours, is often mischaracterized by college and university professors as laziness, irresponsibleness, or immaturity. Students with fixed mindsets often take on only easy tasks, try to make others look dumb, and discount others' achievements to protect their self-image.

10. Jesper Mogensen, a psychologist at the University of Copenhagen, has found that the brain is like a muscle that gets stronger with use and that learning prompts neurons in the brain to grow new connections. You need to understand that you are an agent of your own brain development.

11. When you fail, focus on the strategies you used and the time and effort you put forth to see what caused the failure. Ask for feedback from the teacher. This is a key ingredient in creating a growth mindset.

References

Colvin, G. (2006, October 19). What it takes to be great. *Fortune*. Retrieved from http://money.cnn.com/magazines/fortune/fortune_archive/2006/10/30/8391794/index.htm

Dweck, C. S. (2006). *Mindset: The new psychology of success*. New York: Random House.

Dweck, C. S. (2007a). *Interview in* Stanford News. Retrieved from http://news.stanford.edu/news/2007/february7/videos/179_flash.html

Dweck, C. S. (2007b, November 29). The secret to raising smart kids. *Scientific American*. Retrieved from http://homeworkhelpblog.com/the-secret-to-raising-smartkids/

Dweck, C. S. (2009). Mindset: Powerful insights. *Positive Coaching Alliance*. Retrieved from http://www.positivecoach.org/carol-dweck.aspx

Ferlazzo, L. (2011, June 11). What is the accurate Edison quote on learning from failure? [web post]. Retrieved from http://larryferlazzo.edublogs.org/2011/06/11/what-is-the-accurate-edison-quote-on-learning-from-failure/

Goldberg, E. (2009). *The new executive brain: Frontal lobes in a complex world.* New York: Oxford University Press.

Mogensen, J. (2012). Cognitive recovery and rehabilitation after brain injury: Mechanisms, challenges and support. In A. Agrawal (Ed.), *Brain injury: Functional aspects, rehabilitation and prevention* (pp. 121–150). doi:10.5772/28242

Ratey, J. (2001). *A user's guide to the brain.* New York: Pantheon Books.

Richards, M. (2007, May). *Fixed mindset vs. growth mindset: Which one are you?* Retrieved from http://michaelgr.com/2007/04/15/fixed-mindset-vs-growth-mindset-which-one-are-you/

8

PAYING ATTENTION

Have you ever noticed how hard it is to learn anything when you are bored? When you are interested in something, you will naturally pay attention. When bored, your brain wanders to other topics. With respect to learning, the one law that is absolute is that in order to learn we have to attend to what we are learning. In this chapter we will investigate how the brain pays attention, what draws the brain's attention, and how attention can be improved. Also considered will be the impact that sleep, exercise, and multitasking have on attention, learning, and recall. Most people don't know the significant effects that these three activities have on attention and learning. They can make it either much easier to learn or, unfortunately, much more difficult.

Attention Spans and Learning

How many times have you heard a teacher or your parents say, "I need your full attention"? Even though you might not realize it (and it might be irritating), by requesting your attention, they are helping you to learn. You can learn only when paying attention. Unfortunately, paying attention is not as easy as it might seem. The human brain is wired to attend to whatever is most interesting at a given time and also to hold that focus until something causes it to shift elsewhere. The amount of time before your attention shifts is largely determined by your past experiences; the human brain is influenced after birth by all the experiences that it has. Because each of us has a unique set of experiences, our brains are all wired differently. Even identical twins do not have identical brains because their experiences have been different. This wiring process directly affects your attention span.

If you are under the age of 30, you have lived your entire life in a media-based culture that is full of short bits of information (TV commercials, music videos, text messages, e-mails, tweets, etc.), and constant exposure to these snippets has wired your brain to deal with information that comes at you for shorter periods and on a continual basis. People who lived before today's intense media coverage had brains wired to deal with information given less frequently and over longer periods. For example, new research has shown that the average political sound bite—defined as any footage of a candidate speaking uninterrupted—has dropped to just 8 s (about the time it took you to read this sentence). To give that information some context, consider that during the 1968 presidential election, the average sound bite was a full 43 s. And as recently as the 1990s, in an effort to better promote informed, complex discourse, CBS said it wouldn't broadcast any sound bite less than 30 s. Two decades later we're letting candidates get out only about a third of that before we cut them off (Jefferson, 2011). A person living in the 1850s would experience in their entire lifetime about the same amount of information that you can gain from reading the *New York Times* for one week.

Today, information is so quick and so frequent that brains act in different ways. According to a July 2010 article published in the medical journal *Pediatrics*, increased exposure to television and video games has caused a noticeable decrease in attention spans in school-children (Swing, Gentile, Anderson, & Walsh, 2010). And evidence shows that multitasking (or, more accurately, task shifting), which you have probably been told you are better at than your predecessors, actually damages important alertness capabilities by encouraging you to shift your attention frequently (Wang & Tchernev, 2012). In other words, in our lightning-fast multimedia society, which encourages watching TV, texting friends, and tweeting while studying, the attention span may be an endangered species. And as with any endangered species, special work must be done to nurture and improve your attention span to ensure its survival and, with it, your learning success.

Types of Attention

We know paying attention and holding that attention in order to learn are crucial to college success. But what exactly does it mean to "pay attention." It turns out that researchers disagree about what is meant by the concept of *attention*. The problem arises in determining the kind of attention being used. The research on attention typically refers to focused attention, that is, the very short (perhaps only a few seconds in duration) moment of concentration necessary to address an immediate need, like answering the phone or figuring out what just startled you. This kind of attention has changed little in humans over time. The literature also refers to sustained attention, which is the ability to work on a task over an extended period (Dawson & Medler, 2009). This is the kind of attention most needed in college. The duration of sustained attention has shortened considerably in recent years, making it harder for students to stay focused in class or while doing homework.

The research literature also refers to effortless attention, often referred to as "being in the flow or the zone." This usually occurs while engaged in some challenging but enjoyable activity that involves demands matched by your skills. During such activities, your mind enters a groove of exceptionally focused, and yet effortlessly maintained, attention (Bruya, 2010). You may have experienced this kind of attention while playing a sport or a video game you are skilled at or while on a long run. Although this kind of attention is often not required for academic success, it produces a great feeling when you achieve it.

Finally, there is effortful attention, which is often needed when you study or participate in class. This type of attention is described by the dual-process model of attention and action control theory, which says that to be successful, you have to increase your effort in direct relation to the demands for the control of attention (Osman, 2004). Essentially, as the skills or learning tasks become more difficult, you need to pay more attention in order to understand and learn the material. This is clearly an important kind of attention for college students. Understanding that to learn you have to pay attention and that more difficult learning situations will require you to increase your attention are two keys to your learning success.

Learning, Attention, and Boredom

The author Richard Bach (1977) wrote, "Learning success requires sacrificing boredom and it is not an easy sacrifice to make." Boredom is a choice, but choosing to seek out and engage in an activity when you are bored takes energy. People, books, movies, and professors giving lectures are not inherently boring. Many factors contribute to what you think is boring and what you find interesting, and what you find fascinating may well be boring to someone else. For the most part, humans find things boring if they are too simplistic or too difficult to comprehend. The challenging yet reachable things, in contrast, are typically seen as interesting. Sometimes, when you have to learn material you think is boring, the trick is to find a challenging and interesting aspect of that material.

Have you ever been in what you would describe as an especially boring class? Of course—we all have. The important question is, Did everyone fail that class? Courses in which everyone fails are extremely rare. So, how do students pass a course, perhaps even earn an A, when the material is so boring that paying attention to it is extremely challenging? Typically, successful students put aside their disinterest and force themselves to pay attention because they know they need to learn in spite of the teacher's behavior. It is crucial that you understand that *you do not have the luxury in college to pay attention only to what interests you*. This last statement is so important that it may be the difference between earning academic success and failing out of college. Sometimes, you have to bring meaning and challenge to the material in order to increase your own interest and attention. When it comes to learning, you need greater goals, such as graduation or the feeling of personal accomplishment, to motivate you to pay attention. Remember: the one absolute law of learning is that attention is necessary for learning.

Daydreaming

Some teachers believe that daydreaming students are "slackers" who are not interested in learning. To those teachers, paying attention is fully the responsibility of the student; the teacher plays no role. Studies on the brain and learning paint a different picture. Daydreaming is a normal brain activity. Essentially everyone finds it difficult to stay focused for more than a few minutes on even the easiest tasks, even if the task somehow captures attention (Smallwood & Schooler, 2006). When attention wanes, so does learning; because of this, those who find techniques to improve their ability to pay attention are often the most successful students. We will discuss ways to improve our attention later in this chapter.

Recent research shows that at times mind wandering can be positive, as it allows us to work through some important thinking. Our brains process information to reach goals, some of which are immediate, whereas others are distant. Somehow we have evolved a way to switch between handling the here and now and contemplating long-term objectives (Smallwood & Schooler, 2006). It may be no coincidence that most of the thoughts that people have when they daydream are about the future. Even more telling is the discovery that "zoning out" may be the most fruitful type of mind wandering. When we are no longer aware that our minds are wandering, we may be able to think most deeply about the big picture (Smallwood & Schooler, 2006). So, daydreaming isn't bad; in fact, it is important. However, developing the ability to recognize that you are drifting off at a time when you need to pay attention—in class, for example—is vital to your academic success.

Multitasking

It is almost a badge of honor to say that you are a multitasker in today's world. Being a multitasker is kind of like being a superhero of brainpower. The problem is that multitasking is much more complex than most people realize. When the brain needs to process information, such as when reading, listening in class, or being part of a discussion, it is not possible to attend to two tasks at the same time (Foerde, Knowlton, & Poldrack, 2006). In fact, multitasking violates everything scientists know about how memory works. Imaging studies indicate that memory tasks and distraction stimuli (reading, listening, etc.) engage different parts of the brain and that these regions compete with each other when we try to multitask, causing both tasks to be disrupted (Foerde et al., 2006). Our brain works hard to fool us into thinking it can process information from more than one source at a time. It can't. When trying to do two things at once, the brain temporarily shuts down one task in order to do the other (Dux, Ivanoff, Asplund, & Marois, 2006). For example, when you are texting in class, you temporarily stop listening to the instructor. If you try to do your homework while texting, watching TV, and talking on the phone, you will find it takes much longer to finish your work and you will likely make many more errors. Psychologist Russell Poldrack warned, "We have to be aware that there is a cost to the way that our society is changing, that humans are not built to multitask. We're really built to focus" (as cited in Rosen, 2008, p. 108). Centuries ago "when asked about his particular genius, Isaac Newton responded that if he had made any discoveries, it was 'owing more to patient attention than to any other talent' "(Rosen, 2008, p. 109).

It is possible to multitask in some situations, but generally not in ways that are conducive to learning new material. Just about any new task in which you engage takes a fair amount of concentration at first. This is called controlled or effortful processing. Some things, if practiced extensively, can become easier and easier, to the point that it takes almost no thinking to complete the task. Skiing is a good example of this. When you first start to ski, it is difficult and demands a great deal of attention. After many hours of practice, you can glide down the slopes with little effort; this ease is referred to as automatic processing.

We can multitask two automatic-processing tasks, such as walking (task 1) and humming a familiar song (task 2). At times we can even multitask one automatic task, such as driving, and one controlled task, such as talking to a friend in order to solve a problem.

As great as the human brain is, it is next to impossible to pay attention to two controlled tasks, such as listening to a lecture of material you do not know well and texting a friend, at the same time. When your brain does try to work on two controlled processes at the same time, it must stop attention on one of the tasks in order to start attention on the second task. As mentioned before, this is called task shifting. The bottom line is neuroscience evidence has shown that constant, intentional self-distraction could well be a profound detriment to individual and cultural well-being (Rosen, 2008).

Managing Multiple Tasks

Although we still can't multitask, what we do much more now than in the past is manage multiple tasks. The two concepts are different. Managing multiple tasks is a skill that must be developed, and once developed, it is very valuable. Managing multiple tasks involves appropriately shifting attention, prioritizing resources, and finishing tasks. In fact, many jobs demand successful task managers who can focus their attention on the most important task of the moment and then adapt to changes in task priority as they occur. Think of the emergency room in any big-city hospital (Oberlander, Oswald, Hambrick, & Jones, 2007).

Clearly, the ability to handle tasks quickly is an important skill, and many students are good at this. However, even this form of task management has its drawbacks. Studies by Berman, Jonides, and Kaplan (2008) show that even though people feel entertained, even relaxed, when they are managing many tasks, they're actually fatiguing their brains. The drawback to brain fatigue is that our brains need to engage in direct attention to be in a learning mode. When the brain is fatigued, it is much more difficult to focus. Berman et al. (2008) also found that irritability in people is often caused by brain fatigue.

Task Shifting

When individuals think they are multitasking, they are typically actually engaged in a process called task shifting. Task shifting entails jumping quickly between two or more tasks, at least one of which is controlled to the point that specific cognitive energy is needed. A good example of task shifting is writing a term paper, texting a friend, and watching a television program simultaneously. All three of these tasks are controlled to the point that when one of the tasks is selected for attention, the other two are "shut down." Although your brain will trick you into thinking that task shifting is effective, many studies have shown that it is usually less effective than doing one task at a time. If you focus on your research paper and take breaks to watch television and text your friends, the paper will be of higher quality and you will finish it much more quickly. Researchers have even found that listening to music and studying at the same time can reduce performance. You should listen to music or have the television on while studying only if you need some kind of background sound to keep your brain from being drawn to other sounds in your area. However, for this to work, researchers have found that you must either choose music that is so familiar that it is processed automatically or be sure to cognitively keep the music or television channel in the unattended-to mode; that is, you must ignore the second stimulus. If you are successful, you won't even notice right away if the music happens to stop.

Sleep

Paying attention when you are well rested and interested in the topic is still a challenge given the brain's natural tendency to daydream. Paying attention when you are tired (and sleep deprived) is more than a challenge; it is extremely difficult to do. As we discussed in chapter 2, when the brain is tired or exhausted, it actually shuts down several of the mental processes that are needed for learning. It does this even though you are still awake. In addition, when you do not get enough sleep, the part of your brain that is most important in paying attention and learning new material, called the hippocampus, is unable to ready itself for a new day of learning. This process of clearing away the previous day's unwanted information and passing the important information to the neocortex for memory processing requires a full night's rest (7.5–9 hr). To be ready to pay attention, you must find a way to get enough sleep; otherwise, you are making new learning difficult.

Exercise

As discussed in chapter 3, research clearly shows that people who engage in regular aerobic exercise get a significant boost in their ability to pay attention. This is because the neurochemicals norepinephrine, dopamine, and serotonin are released in the brain in larger amounts when you exercise, and these neurochemicals, especially norepinephrine, enhance your ability to pay attention, focus, concentrate, and be motivated to learn (Ratey, 2008). In addition, exercise makes the body healthy and promotes good sleep, which are both important in enhancing your ability to pay attention. Doing aerobic exercise (which is the gold standard) or any exercise four to five days a week is one of the best ways to improve your ability to pay attention and learn.

"Easy" Ways to Increase Attention

The Internet is full of suggestions for increasing your attention span and improving your concentration. However, many of these suggestions are not rooted in science. A 2010 evaluation of purported ways to maintain or improve cognitive function, including attention, conducted for the National Institutes of Health, found many of the claims to be unsupported (Begley, 2011). For example, vitamins B6, B12, and E; beta carotene; folic acid; and the trendy antioxidants called flavonoids were found to have no value in boosting attention or cognitive functioning. Also, claims that alcohol, omega-3s (the fatty acids in fish), and large social networks improve brain function were found to be weak (Begley, 2011).

There is some solid scientific research, however, in the area of enhancing attention. Among a sample group of people who meditated on a regular basis for six months, meditation was shown to increase the thickness of brain regions that control attention and process sensory signals from the outside world (Jha, 2011). In the same group, meditation was also shown to enhance mental agility and attention by changing brain structure and function so that brain processes were more efficient, a quality that is associated with higher intelligence (Jha, 2011). Other studies have similarly demonstrated the positive health benefits of meditation, including lowered stress levels (Nidich et al., 2009).

Strategies for Enhancing Attention

There are a variety of ways to improve your attention span. Some require little effort and are easy to implement. Check out the suggestions that follow:

1. Write yourself a message. This may sound silly, but it works. Writing yourself a note and keeping it in a place where you can see it all the time (e.g., on the cover of your notebook or textbook) will remind you to stay on task and pay attention in class.
2. Fix your environment. If you need to pay attention, then eliminate distractions. Go to the library or study room or find an empty classroom. Turn off your phone (it will be okay, really). In the classroom, if possible, sit by students who pay attention and avoid those who are chatty.
3. Record lectures. If you have a recording of a lecture, you can stop and start the lecture at your own convenience, when you are ready to pay attention.
4. Focus on the bigger goal. We went to college, and we know that classes can sometimes be boring or seem irrelevant. Keep your eye on the bigger goals of graduation and developing your full potential as a way to force yourself to pay attention.

Divide and Conquer

In the end, the best ways to improve your attention are sleep, exercise, and self-control. Attention requires effort and a desire to stay focused. In addition, it is often easier to focus and stay attentive to a task if you have a goal in mind. For example, if the task is large (such as reading an 80-page chapter), it is easier to stay focused if you divide the task into manageable parts, say, 20 pages at a time, and allow yourself a break. It is easy to get overwhelmed by the amount of work that can be required in college, and as a result, you might become distracted by the size of the task—"How am I ever going to get this done?" Focusing on what is doable will help keep you on task and reduce your sense of being overwhelmed.

A Final Thought

The famous biologist and expert on learning James Zull (2002) writes,

> Paying attention does not mean unrelenting attention on one focal point. . . . The brain is more likely to notice details when it scans than when it focuses. . . . It seems then, that instead of asking people to pay attention, we might ask them to look at things from many different angles. Instead of sitting still, we might ask them to move around so they can see details. (pp. 142–143)

Chapter Summary

It would be wonderful if you were interested in everything you were required to learn. If you had only interesting classes with interesting teachers, paying attention would be easy to do. However, school is at times challenging, difficult, and not all that interesting. Because you learn only what you pay attention to, you must use the information from this chapter to improve your ability to pay attention. As noted at the beginning of the chapter, maintaining focus is not always easy. It requires preparing yourself to learn with the proper sleep, diet, and exercise. It requires recognizing when you are daydreaming and bringing your attention back to the task at hand. And it requires ramping up your attention when the learning becomes more challenging. If you follow the suggestions in this chapter, you should be able to improve your ability to pay attention. Following are the key ideas from this chapter:

1. Attention is absolutely necessary for learning.
2. A person's attention span changes from situation to situation but is greatly affected by the culture in which he or she lives. Studies suggest many people under the age of 30 may have attention spans as short as 10 min.
3. Your brain has limitations in terms of how many things it can focus on at the same time.
4. When you are task shifting, it takes longer to complete a task and your work likely contains more errors.
5. Everyone daydreams. It is a natural part of the brain's planning and problem-solving process.
6. Getting enough sleep is crucial to being able to pay attention in class.
7. Aerobic exercise improves attention.

References

Bach, R. (1977). *Illusions: The adventures of a reluctant messiah.* New York: Dell.

Begley, S. (2011, January 3). Can you build a better brain? *Newsweek.* Retrieved from http://www.thedailybeast.com/newsweek/2011/01/03/can-you-build-a-better-brain.html

Berman, M., Jonides, J., & Kaplan, S. (2008, December). The cognitive benefits of interacting with nature. *Psychological Science, 19,* 1207–1212.

Bruya, B. (2010). *Effortless attention: A new perspective on the cognitive science of attention and action.* Cambridge, MA: MIT Press.

Dawson, M., & Medler, D. (2009). Sustained attention. In *Dictionary of cognitive science.* Retrieved from http://www.bcp.psych.ualberta.ca/~mike/Pearl_Street/Dictionary/contents/S/sustained_attention.html

Dux, P. E., Ivanoff, J., Asplund, C. L. O., & Marois, R. (2006). Isolation of a central bottleneck of information processing with time-resolved fMRI. *Neuron, 52*(6), 1109–1120.

Foerde, K., Knowlton, B., & Poldrack, R. (2006). Modulation of competing memory systems by distraction. *Proceedings of the National Academy of Science, 103,* 11778–11783.

Jefferson, C. (2011, January 4). Sound bites catch up to attention spans. *Good. is*. Retrieved from http://www.good.is/posts/attention-spans-tv-sound-bit es-both-getting-shorter/

Jha, A. (2011). Meditation improves brain anatomy and function. *Psychiatry Research: Neuroimaging, 191*(1), 1–86.

Nidich, S. I., Fields, J. Z., Rainforth, M. V., Pomerantz, R., Cella, D., Kristeller J., . . . Schneider, R. H. (2009). A randomized controlled trial of the effects of transcendental meditation on quality of life in older breast cancer patients. *Integrative Cancer Therapies, 8*(3), 228–234.

Oberlander, E., Oswald, F., Hambrick, D., & Jones, L. (2007). *Individual difference variables as predictors of error during multitasking* (NPRST/ BUPERS-1). Millington, TN: Bureau of Naval Personnel, Navy Personnel Research, Studies, and Technology Division.

Osman, M. (2004). An evaluation of dual-process theories of reasoning. *Psychonomic Bulletin & Review, 11*(6), 988–1010.

Ratey, J. (2008). *Spark: The revolutionary new science of exercise and the brain.* New York: Little, Brown.

Rosen, C. (2008). Myth of multitasking. *New Atlantis.* Retrieved from http:// www.thenewatlantis.com/publications/the-myth-of-multitasking

Smallwood, J., & Schooler, J. (2006). The restless mind. *Psychological Bulletin, 132*(6), 946–958.

Swing, E., Gentile, D., Anderson, C., & Walsh, D. (2010, June). Television and video game exposure and the development of attention problems. *Pediatrics, 126*(2), 214–221. doi:10.1542/peds.2009-1508

Wang, Z., & Tchernev, J. (2012). The "myth" of media multitasking: Recip-rocal dynamics of media multitasking, personal needs, and gratifications. *Journal of Communication, 62*(3), 493–513. Retrieved from http://onlineli brary.wiley.com/doi/10.1111/j.1460-2466.2012.01641.x/pdf

Zull, J. (2002). *The art of changing the brain.* Sterling, VA: Stylus.

9

A MESSAGE FROM THE AUTHORS

One of the great benefits that a college student today has over previous generations of college students has come from the development of neuroimaging tools that allow, for the first time in human history, scientists to look inside the human brain and see how it operates. As a result, today's students have accurate, scientifically proven information about how their brains learn and remember information and skills, whereas those who came before just had to guess. What we have tried to do in this book is guide you through the new evidence and techniques in a way that makes it easy for you to implement them in your own life. The information in this book is not our opinion but rather scientific fact about what actions work and should be integrated into your daily life as a student and lifelong learner. The basic finding that we have reinforced throughout this book is that *the one who does the work does the learning*. There is, unfortunately, no magic pill that you can take to make learning easy. The brain can hang on to new learning it encounters every day only by hard work and continual practice. We believe that by implementing the information discussed in this book, you will be maximizing your brain's ability to learn, and that is all anyone can ask of you.

Employment and College Success

In 1973 only 28% of jobs in the United States required a college degree. A new Georgetown University study indicates that by 2018 that number will be close to 55–65% depending on the state you live in (Carnevale, Smith, & Strohl, 2010). A college degree and a set of learning skills that will allow you to compete in the world marketplace are more important than ever before. Add to this change in employment expectations the extraordinary pace of change and growth of knowledge in the world you live in (and will live in for the next 80 years or so), and you have a clear picture of why you need to learn in harmony with your brain. From the beginning of time until 2003, humankind collected an estimated 5 exabytes of data (5 exabytes = 1 quintillion bytes). Humans now collect 5 exabytes of data every two days, and it is expected that within two years they will collect the same amount every few minutes (Tapscott, 2011). Learning to manage your life when faced with this kind of data explosion will require a brain that is optimized to learn.

Becoming a Lifelong Learner

Most of you reading this book are part of the first generation for which having a college degree will be only the starting point of your life as a learner. Your ability to use your college experience to not only earn a degree but also become a successful lifelong learner, capable of updating skills and knowledge as needed, will be a significant determiner of your long-term success. The U.S. Department of Labor estimates that if you are 18 years old today, you will have 10–14 different jobs by the time you are 38, and each job will require new knowledge and skills. One of the hopes we had in writing this book was to help you in some small way prepare for this extraordinary future.

Time and Practice

One of the most important messages in this book is that learning anything new takes more time, practice, and skill than people think. The human brain strengthens memories each time they are recalled. The more often a task or skill is practiced, the stronger the memory for that task or skill becomes. There is no substitute for practice over time if you want to learn something new successfully. The more ways you use the information (elaboration, discussed in chapter 6) and the more times you recall the information, the greater the likelihood that you will be able to recall the information or skill when you need it. Knowing how long-term memories are formed and acting accordingly can lead to long-term learning success.

Preparing to Learn

The human brain is an amazing, complex, and beautiful organ, but it needs to be cared for with sleep, hydration, nutrition, and exercise for it to operate at its best. When you have prepared your brain to learn by getting 7.5–9 hr of sleep each night, engaging in aerobic exercise four to five times a week, and making certain that you are hydrated and well fed, then you are truly prepared to learn. This preparation is an additional responsibility that you must be willing to take on. Prior generations didn't know how important these four actions were to their brain's ability to learn, so for them, preparation was making sure they had pants on when they left for class. With new discoveries come new opportunities and responsibilities. Preparing your brain for learning is crucial to your college and lifelong success.

Money Matters

College graduates have known for decades that their degree would almost always provide access to higher-paying jobs and greater opportunities. Recent studies show that the income gap between those with only a high school diploma and college graduates is widening. People who complete college and continue to update their skills and knowledge in order to remain productive in their careers have income levels that are two to four times higher over a lifetime than those of people who earn only a high school diploma. Maximizing your brain's learning

abilities so that you can compete in the job market will play a significant role in what happens to you over the course of your lifetime.

What Is Not in This Book

In writing this book, we made a conscious decision not to include information about study strategies or study skills. We did this not because
these are not important tools and skills but rather because there are an
endless number of fine websites and books that already exist that can
suggest strategies you might find helpful in aiding your learning and
studying activities. One excellent site is http://faculty.bucks.edu/spec
pop/topics.htm. You will also find excellent help on your own campus,
as every college now has student academic support centers where help
in choosing the right study or learning strategy is just a phone call or
an e-mail away.

We also decided not to fully address the social and emotional issues
that play a significant role in helping or interfering with learning for
similar reasons. Social and emotional factors have a profound impact on
the learning process. Note, for example, the role stress plays in memory,
as discussed in chapter 6. We know that your college experience is also
about learning how to deal with yourself, others, and relationships in
an effective manner; developing affective tools, such as sympathy and
empathy for others; and maintaining positive relationships. We believe
these issues are important, and we know that much has already been
written about their role in enhancing or deterring effective learning. For
example, using study groups or peer-group learning, finding a mentor,
and being involved in a campus organization that allows you to learn
leadership skills or enhance your cooperation skills are all important
to your overall learning experience. There is significant evidence that
collaborative learning activities often lead to enhanced understanding
and exposure to new insights and views that will be lost if one works
solely alone. We also recognize that learning to develop a set of values
and ideas that will guide your life is also part of a complete college
experience. In the appendix we have provided a few excellent resources
that might help you in developing these social and emotional skills.

Just as all campuses have resources for helping with study skills and strategies, all colleges also have numerous organizations and support systems in place to help students develop their social and emotional skill set, and we encourage you to use them.

A Final Thought: Find Balance in Your Life

Your life in college and after will be filled with challenges that will require a brain that is optimized for learning, but your brain is not the only thing that will matter. To find success in college and in life, you need to find a balance between the demands of academic life and the joys, pleasures, and people that make your life meaningful. What we wish for you is that you find balance in all aspects of your life—your sleep, exercise, diet, social life, emotional health, and academic endeavors— and that you remember to learn in harmony with your brain.

References

Carnevale, A. P., Smith, N., & Strohl, J. (2010, June). *Projections of jobs and education requirements through 2018*. Washington, DC: Georgetown University, Center for Education and the Workforce. Retrieved from http://www9.georgetown.edu/grad/gppi/hpi/cew/pdfs/FullReport.pdf

Tapscott, D. (2011). What scientific concept would improve everybody's cognitive toolkit? *Edge*. Retrieved from http://edge.org/response-detail/10586

APPENDIX

Cooperation and Teamwork

In his 1990 book *The Evolution of Cooperation*, social scientist Robert Axelrod wrote, "Cooperation involves mutual reciprocity." Axelrod goes on to say, "There may always be an element of self-interest in any cooperative endeavor, as well as a concern for others or for the welfare of the group as a whole" (Axelrod, 1990).

Collaboration is built from trust and mutual respect along with a willingness to accept others' differences and quirks. Keeping the bigger picture of accomplishing the task in mind at all times is the key to success. To read more about cooperation and teamwork visit http://ows.edb.utexas.edu/site/computer-supported-collaborative-learning-2011/6-social-aspects-learning-cscl.

Peer Study Groups

Study groups typically involve four to six students who meet weekly, sometimes more often, to share information, knowledge, and expertise about a course in which they are all enrolled. The study group environment offers students an opportunity to engage in a more in-depth discussion about course material. Students working in small groups typically learn more of what is taught and retain it longer than they would in other instructional formats. To learn more about study groups visit www.umich.edu/~lsastudy/peers.html.

Group Study Guidelines

Often college is seen as a competitive place, so we tend to overlook the power of cooperation. The power of groups is widely accepted in the business world and can easily be used in your job as a student in the form of a study group. For a list of guidelines for group study visit www.d.umn.edu/kmc/student/loon/acad/strat/grpstudy1.html.

Finding a Mentor

Having a good mentor can be extremely helpful when you're looking for career advice, job opportunities, or even a role model who's already succeeded at something you'd like to do. Read more about finding a mentor at www.huffingtonpost.com/her-campus/post_3086_b_1324 242.html.

Living a Balanced Life

A well-balanced life is essential for personal effectiveness, peace of mind, and living well. There is always someone, or something, to answer to. There are things we want to do and things we must do. The challenge is to balance what we must do with what we enjoy and want to do. This is not always easy. Tips for living a balanced life are available at www .essentiallifeskills.net/wellbalancedlife.html.

Reference

Axelrod, R. (1990). *The evolution of cooperation*. London: Penguin Books.

INDEX

Also by Terry Doyle

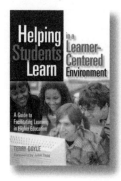

Helping Students Learn in a Learner-Centered Environment
A Guide to Facilitating Learning in Higher Education
Foreword by John Tagg

"Oh boy, am I glad this book is here. Terry Doyle has explored and integrated a wide range of literature on learning. His book brings together findings that will enable us to answer what so many college & university faculty members want to know: How do we enable our students to learn to learn (and love it)? If your goal is to develop lifelong learners, this book is a guidebook for your practice."

—Laurie Richlin,
Director, Faculty Development,
Charles R. Drew University of Medicine and Science

Learner Centered Teaching
Putting the Research on Learning into Practice
Foreword by Todd Zakrajsek

"Doyle's latest book offers new and compelling contributions to the literature on learner-centered teaching (LCT). Drawing on research from neuroscience, biology, and cognitive psychology, his topics include convincing students to do the work, using authentic learning, sharing power, teaching to all senses, and emphasizing patterns, repetition, and exercise. A final chapter convinces others to embrace LCT. Doyle's relevant examples include his own conversion as a reading teacher. His clear explanations lead to practical classroom applications."

—Barbara J. Millis,
The University of Texas at San Antonio

22883 Quicksilver Drive
Sterling, VA 20166-2102   Subscribe to our e-mail alerts: www.Styluspub.com